Top
Heavy

Top
Heavy

The Increasing Inequality of Wealth in America and What Can Be Done About It

A NEWLY UPDATED AND
EXPANDED EDITION OF A
CENTURY FOUNDATION REPORT

Edward N. Wolff

THE NEW PRESS
NEW YORK

Published in the United States by The New Press, New York, 2002
Distributed by W. W. Norton & Company, Inc., New York

LIBRARY OF CONGRESS CATALOGING-IN-PUBLICATION DATA

Wolff, Edward N.
Top heavy: the increasing inequality of wealth in America and what can be done about it /
Edward N. Wolff.—Updated and expanded ed.
p. cm.
A newly updated and expanded edition of a Century Foundation report.
Includes bibliographical references and index.
ISBN 1-56584-665-6 (pbk.)
1. Wealth tax—United States. 2. Income distribution—United States. I. Twentieth Century
Fund. II. Title.
HJ4120.W65 2002
336.24'2—dc21   2001044123

Top Heavy is an expanded edition of a Century Foundation (formerly the Twentieth Century Fund) study. The Century Foundation sponsors and supervises timely analyses of economic policy, foreign affairs, and domestic political issues. Not-for-profit and nonpartisan, it was founded in 1919 and endowed by Edward A. Filene.

The New Press was established in 1990 as a not-for-profit alternative to the large, commercial publishing houses currently dominating the book publishing industry. The New Press operates in the public interest rather than for private gain, and is committed to publishing, in innovative ways, works of educational, cultural, and community value that are often deemed insufficiently profitable.

The New Press, 450 West 41st Street, 6th floor, New York, NY 10036
www.thenewpress.com

Book design by Lovedog Studio

Printed in the United States of America

2 4 6 8 10 9 7 5 3

Contents

Foreword

Americans, by and large, believe that they have created a society second to none when it comes to democracy and opportunity. The American experience in these areas has been dynamic. Starting two centuries ago from a relatively narrow base of full citizenship and full participation in the economy, increasing numbers of citizens have been able to gain admission to the mainstream, obtaining everything from the basic right to vote to the opportunity to attend the best of colleges or to become a member of an admired profession. Of course, progress has not been smooth—and there have been setbacks—but the trend generally has been toward greater democracy and greater opportunity for all. Although on many occasions we have reinvented ourselves through immigration and have restructured our economy, over time we have come to see the resulting mix as one that is as classically American as, say, apple pie—but, come to think of it, as one that no longer qualifies as our favorite dessert.

The truth is that, for all our pride and even triumphalism about what we have accomplished, there is plenty of evidence that Americans are not completely happy with the current state of the nation. Democracy in the United States suffers from low voter participation and unprecedented reliance on campaign money. In fact, it is fair to say that today public frustration and anger about representative democracy is acute. A large number of citizens believe that they can rely on neither a fair count of their votes on election day nor the numbers in the decennial census. Moreover, the American economy, for all its recent successes, looks a little fragile when one considers that private debt in the nation is at an all-time high and the stock market seems a good deal less like a sure thing. No wonder—we are a nation of worriers, never completely satisfied with what we have, even when it may be the best the world has to offer.

Underlying much of our present uneasiness is a widespread concern that America offers less opportunity to young people today than it did to those in past generations. For this, some blame international competition and immigration, some the education system, and some the government itself. Disquietingly, the evidence supports, at least in part, the perception of diminished prospects for average citizens and their families.

Over the past decade, many studies have established that the working population of the United States—especially men with less than a college education—are not only doing more poorly than their parents but are seeing their real wages decline. Between 1947 and 1973, American families in every income category enjoyed income growth—and the poorest families had the highest rate of all. Then, between 1973 and 1998, income remained close to stagnant (adjusted for inflation) for the bottom 40 percent of families, growing robustly only for the top quarter. Indeed, in 1993, before the boom that followed, the bottom half of families were worse off than in 1973.

These issues were just reaching public awareness in January 1995 when the Twentieth Century Fund (now the Century Foundation) released the first edition of *Top Heavy* by Edward N. Wolff, professor of economics at New York University. A second edition, with evidence that reinforced the continuing nature of inequality, was published by The New Press in 1996. Now, for 2002, Wolff has prepared a third edition of his work, updating his research with the latest statistics available at the close of the twentieth century. The added data and fresh analysis add greatly to our knowledge of trends in income and wealth distribution. While wealth inequality has always been—and continues to be—greater than income inequality, Wolff has documented truly remarkable increases in wealth inequality over the years. During the 1980s, the top 1 percent of wealth holders enjoyed two-thirds of all increases in financial wealth. The bottom 80 percent of households ended up with less real financial wealth in 1989 than in 1983. Startlingly, Wolff reported that during the 1980s the United States had gone from a position of less wealth inequality among its citizens than in Europe to one of greater wealth inequality than is found in those class-ridden societies. In fact, not one of the countries with comparable data— France, Germany, Japan, Sweden, or Canada—has wealth distributed as unequally as this nation does.

In each of these editions, there has been little good news in Wolff's research when it comes to African Americans. The median wealth of nonwhite citizens actually fell during the 1980s, though it rose in the 1990s. And while the black-white wealth gap narrowed in the 1990s, the median white household still has eight times as much wealth as the median black household. It may be fashionable to look past such unpleasant information, but Wolff has made an important contribution by simply forcing his readers to react to the eloquence of the facts.

From the facts, Wolff moves to policy. In this volume he once again offers a bold and carefully documented proposal to impose a wealth tax, similar to that in place in many European countries. Taking as his model the modest tax in effect in Switzerland, Wolff estimates that such a levy in the United States would produce $52 billion annually. Under his proposal, even the wealthiest families would pay a lower rate than the management fees of a typical mutual fund, and three-quarters of Americans would pay practically nothing.

Wolff's proposal continues to confound the (literally) "politically correct" notion that says we must ignore growing inequality and exclude from consideration tax policy options that attempt to ameliorate the situation. Indeed, as of this writing, there is a substantial possibility of new tax cuts that generally favor the wealthiest citizens.

At the Century Foundation, we are convinced that alternatives are worth exploring, especially when, as is the case with Wolff's work, they are backed by solid and compelling research. Certainly, it remains important for Americans to understand the forces that call into question the success of our commitment to democracy and economic opportunity. With a remarkably large segment of the population standing still or even losing ground in terms of wealth and income, the inevitably greater insecurity this group faces should be considered as one possible cause of the anger that periodically shakes our democratic system.

When the first edition of *Top Heavy* was released, Wolff's findings crystallized the growing interest in this issue and sparked a sharp and widespread controversy. Conservatives led the effort to discredit his work, holding fast to the notion that the years of the two Reagan administrations and the consequences of supply-side economics created a rising tide that had lifted all boats. But, as increasing numbers of independent scholars came forth on Wolff's side of the argument, the weight of evidence and informed opinion essentially swamped the assertions of the critics. Put simply, Wolff's patient research and solid conclusions wound up convincing virtually all objective commentators.

Since the first edition, there have been many changes in the economic circumstances of America and its citizens, but clearly the overall picture remains perplexing. Wealth inequality in America is still dramatic and persistent. Given the heavy concentration of stock ownership among the country's richest citizens, even a return to the bull market conditions of the 1990s is unlikely to alter the disturbing trends of the past three decades.

Looking back, neither political rhetoric nor laissez-faire bromides have had any effect on this phenomenon. One thing, however, is obvious: We are unlikely to have either the society or the economy we want until there is a reversal in the pattern of growing income and wealth inequality in the United States. Edward Wolff's work is important because it ensures that our understanding of these issues is grounded in rigorous analysis.

Thanks to The New Press, *Top Heavy* will continue to inform the ongoing debate about the state of the American economy. On behalf of the trustees of the Century Foundation, I thank Professor Wolff for his willingness to keep his research relevant and evergreen.

Richard C. Leone, President
The Century Foundation

1

Introduction

Many people are aware that income inequality has increased over the past twenty years. Upper-income groups have continued to do well decade after decade, while others, particularly those without a college degree, and especially the young, have seen their real income decline. The *1994 Economic Report of the President* referred to the 1979–90 fall in real income of men with only four years of high school (a 21 percent decline) as "stunning."[1] The picture has not changed much since 1994. The real income of this group is still down by 9 percent since 1979.[2] Indeed, these changes in income distribution constitute one of the strongest arguments against the tax cut measures proposed by President George W. Bush in January 2001. Those at the top of the income distribution who are being offered additional tax relief are the very people whose incomes grew most rapidly.

This paper broadens the discussion of distribution and taxation to include something that usually is neglected: wealth. Almost all discussions of distributional issues have centered on income.

Income in any year is a measure of a household's economic position, but it can vary greatly from year to year. A high income still can leave a household vulnerable. A better indicator of long-run economic security is wealth—the net worth of the household. Wealth is found by (1) adding together the current value of all the assets a household owns: financial wealth such as bank accounts, stocks, bonds, life insurance savings, mutual fund shares; houses and unincorporated businesses; consumer durables such as cars and major appliances; and the value of pension rights, and (2) subtracting liabilities: consumer debt, mortgage balances, other outstanding debt. Wealth can vary from year to year as asset prices rise and fall, but it remains the foundation of a family's long-term security. Without wealth, a family lives from hand to mouth, no matter how high its income.

Examination of the data on wealth distribution leads to a disturbing question: Is America still the land of opportunity? The growing divergence evident in income distribution is even starker in wealth distribution. Equalizing trends during the 1930s through the 1970s reversed sharply in the 1980s. The gap between haves and have-nots is greater now—at the start of the twenty-first century—than at any time since 1929. The sharp increase in inequality since the late 1970s has made wealth distribution in the United States more unequal than it is in what used to be perceived as the class-ridden societies of northwestern Europe.

Contrary to popular perception, the go-go years of the 1980s and 1990s did not offer everyone a piece of the action. They were a party for those at the very top of the wealth distribution. While those in the fast lane enjoyed large increases in wealth over the two decades, the wealth of much of the rest of the population did not simply grow more slowly; it actually fell. Looking at real financial wealth alone—including bank accounts, stocks, and bonds, but excluding durable goods, housing, and pension wealth—the average holdings of the bottom 40 percent of households stayed negative throughout the period from 1983 to 1998. Adding in housing wealth makes the picture somewhat less grim, with the average holdings of the bottom 40 percent turning positive, but this group still had less wealth in 1998 than in 1983. The 1990s also saw an explosion in the number of millionaires and multimillionaires. The number of households worth $1,000,000 or more grew by almost 60 percent; the number worth $10,000,000 or more almost quadrupled.

Not surprisingly, in light of these facts, the racial distribution of wealth deteriorated in the 1980s and 1990s, from an already unacceptable level. Relative income of African-American households held steady at about 60 percent of white income in the 1980s and 1990s, and the relative wealth position of black families failed to progress. Historically, black wealth always has been much lower than that of whites—the legacy of slavery, discrimination, and low incomes. But between 1983 and 1998, a bad situation grew worse. In 1983, the average wealth of white families was 5.3 times that of African-American families. In 1998, the ratio was back up to 5.5. Middle-class black households did succeed in narrowing the wealth gap with whites, but most nonwhite families moved even further behind. More than one in four African-American households now have no positive wealth at all, in contrast to one in seven white households.

These trends suggest that for reasons of fairness, the United States should consider broad taxation of wealth. Currently, we tax wealth in several specific ways. Our most important wealth tax, the property tax, is administered at the state and local level and is beyond the scope of this study. At the federal level, wealth is taxed through the capital gains tax and, at death, through estate taxes. But eleven other Organization for Economic Cooperation and Development (OECD) countries have additional taxes on wealth. By studying these taxes and employing computer simulation, it is possible to assess the revenue effects and distributional implications that would be obtained were, for example, the tax systems of Germany, Sweden, or Switzerland to be adopted in the United States.

Although wealth taxation in one form or another is ubiquitous in rich countries, nowhere is it a major revenue source—that is, more than a small percentage of total revenue. The international mobility of financial wealth and widespread concern about the negative incentive effects of wealth taxation—against saving and for capital flight—as well as the power of affluent elites all work to reduce the level of effective taxation. Nevertheless, even a very simple and modest tax like Switzerland's could raise substantial revenues in the United States. A wealth tax modeled on Switzerland's—with an $83,000 exclusion and a top rate for the wealthiest of three-tenths of 1 percent—would generate an estimated $52 billion annually. This is not much when measured against total federal revenues, to say nothing of total income or wealth. Nevertheless, it is significant in the context of the debates surrounding the budgets proposed by President Bush. A wealth tax offers us an important new fiscal option. It could be used to help finance any of the many needs of our society, from highway and bridge repair to environmental cleanup to health care to prisons. Or it could be used to replace other taxes that are deemed less fair or entail more damaging economic disincentives. And while any new tax would bring howls from the antitax lobby, given the concentration of financial wealth, it would be hard to find a lot of people who would be directly affected. Even the wealthiest households could be expected to pay less than 10 percent of the annual real return on their capital as their new wealth tax liability; more than three-quarters of all families would pay practically nothing. Would such a tax have terrible supply-side effects? Well, one might ask whether Switzerland suffers from capital flight and impoverishment.

2

Why Wealth?

Before exploring more closely the facts and policies surrounding wealth inequality, a review of the central concepts is helpful. Family wealth refers to the net dollar value of the stock of assets less liabilities (or debt) held by a household at one point in time.[1] Income, in contrast, refers to a flow of dollars over a period of time, usually a year. Though certain forms of income are derived from wealth, such as interest from savings accounts and bonds, dividends from stock shares, and rent from real estate, income and wealth are by no means identical. Many kinds of income—wages and salaries, food stamps and other transfer payments—are not derived from household wealth, and many forms of wealth, such as owner-occupied housing, produce no corresponding cash income flow.

Most people think of family income as a measure of well-being, but family wealth is also a source of well-being, independent of the direct income it provides. There are both narrowly economic and broader reasons for the importance of wealth. Some assets, particularly owner-occupied housing, provide services directly to the owner. This is also true for consumer durables, such as automobiles. Such assets can substitute for financial income in satisfying economic needs. Families receiving the same financial income but differing in their stocks of housing and consumer durables will experience different levels of well-being.

More important, perhaps, than its role as a source of income is the security that wealth brings to its owners, who know that their consumption can be sustained even if income fluctuates. Most assets can be sold for cash or used as collateral for loans, thus providing for unanticipated consumption needs. In times of economic stress, occasioned by such crises as unemployment, sickness, or family breakup, wealth is an important cushion. The very knowledge that wealth is at hand is a source of comfort for many families.

In the political arena, large fortunes can be a source of economic power and social influence that is not directly captured in the measure of annual income. Large accumulations of financial and business assets can confer special privileges on their holders. Such fortunes are often transmitted to succeeding generations, thus creating family "dynasties."

In most households, wealth varies from year to year. First, saving out of current income may augment wealth, just as spending in excess of income may diminish it. Second, assets already held by the family may change in value.[2] Finally, gifts and inheritances from or to a family member may change household wealth.

It is apparent that a family's wealth can be expected to depend on the age of its members because older working individuals generally will have spent more years saving and accumulating assets. Indeed, wealth, like income, is related to age, but the relationship is not a strong one since savings rates, the rate of return on asset holdings, and gifts and inheritances will generally differ among families of similar age profile, even when they have the same earnings history.

Wealth and income are positively correlated (that is, families with more income generally have more wealth), but this association, too, is far from perfect.[3] One reason is that rates of return on various components of wealth vary widely between years and within any one year.[4] Even well-reported asset and income data would yield an incomplete picture of the wealth from which they flow.[5] Other types of wealth, as noted earlier, may yield no income at all in a given year. Age explains part of the variation of the wealth-income ratio, but much is left unaccounted for.[6] As a result of this unexplained variability, wealth measures well-being differently from annual income, in both relative and absolute terms.

Household Wealth Inequality in the United States: Present Level and Historical Trends

Wealth inequality in the United States was at a seventy-year high in 1998 (the latest date available), with the top 1 percent of wealth holders controlling 38 percent of total household wealth. If we focus more narrowly, on financial wealth, the richest 1 percent of households owned 47 percent of the total. How did this come to pass? After the stock market crash of 1929, there ensued a gradual if somewhat erratic reduction in wealth inequality, which seems to have lasted until the late 1970s. Since then, inequality of wealth holdings, like that of income, has risen sharply (see Figure 3-1).[1] If Social Security and other types of pension wealth ("augmented wealth") are included, the improvement between 1929 and 1979 appears greater, but the increase in inequality since 1980 is still sharply in evidence.

The rise in wealth inequality from 1983 to 1998 (a period for which there is comparable detailed household survey information) is particularly striking. The share of the top 1 percent of wealth holders rose by 5 percent. The wealth of the bottom 40 percent

FIGURE 3–1

SHARE OF WEALTH OWNED BY THE TOP 1 PERCENT OF HOUSEHOLDS IN THE UNITED STATES, 1922–1998

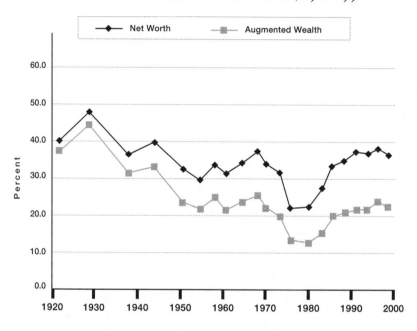

showed an absolute decline. Almost all the absolute gains in real wealth accrued to the top 20 percent of wealth holders.

CHANGES IN AVERAGE WEALTH HOLDINGS

Look first at trends in real wealth over the period from 1962 to 1998 (all in 1998 dollars).[2] As Figure 3-2 shows, average wealth grew at a respectable pace from 1962 to 1983 and even faster from 1983 to 1989. By 1989, the average wealth of households was $244,000 (in 1998 dollars), almost two-thirds higher than in 1962. From 1989 to 1998, wealth grew more slowly. In fact, mean marketable wealth grew only about half as fast between 1989 and 1998 as between 1983 and 1989 (1.2 percent per year versus 2.3 percent). Still, by 1998, average wealth had reached $270,000.

FIGURE 3-2

ANNUAL RATE OF CHANGE IN REAL INCOME AND WEALTH
1962–1983, 1983–1989, AND 1989–1998

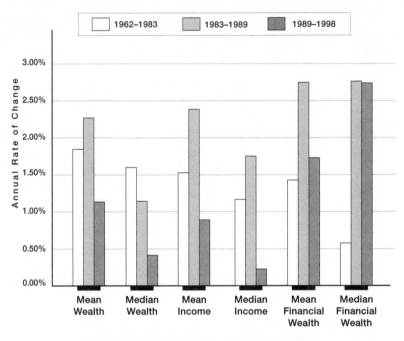

Source: 1962, from the Survey of Financial Characteristics of Consumers;
1983, 1989, and 1998, from the Survey of Consumer Finances

Average financial wealth grew faster than marketable wealth in the 1983–89 period (2.7 versus 2.3 percent per year), reflecting the increased importance of bank deposits, financial assets, equities, and small businesses in the overall household portfolio over this period. This reversed the relationship of the 1962–83 period, when financial wealth grew more slowly than marketable wealth (1.4 versus 1.8 percent per year). In the 1989–98 period, the gain in average financial wealth again outstripped net worth (1.7 versus 1.2 percent per year).

Average household income also grew faster in the 1983–89 period than in the 1962–83 period. Its annual growth accelerated from

1.5 percent to 2.4. Whereas in the first of the two periods, average income grew more slowly than average wealth (a difference of 0.3 percentage points per year), in the latter it grew slightly faster (a difference of 0.1 percentage points per year). However, in the 1989–98 period, income growth plummeted to 0.9 percent per year (0.2 percentage points per year lower than wealth growth).

The robust growth of average wealth disguises some changes in the distribution of that wealth. This becomes clear after examination of median rather than mean wealth. Mean wealth is simply the average: total wealth divided by total number of households. If the wealth of only the top 20 percent of households increases (with nothing else changing), then mean wealth increases because total wealth increases.[3] In contrast, the median of wealth distribution is defined as the level of wealth that divides the population of households into two equal-sized groups (those with more wealth than the median and those with less). Returning to the earlier example, if only the top quintile enjoys an increase in wealth, median wealth is unaffected even though mean wealth increases, because all additional wealth accrues to people well above the median income. The median tracks what is happening in the middle of wealth distribution.[4] When trends in the mean deviate from trends in the median, this is a signal that gains and losses are unevenly distributed.

The trend in median household wealth in the United States gives a contrasting picture to the growth of mean wealth. Unlike mean marketable wealth, median marketable wealth grew faster in the 1962–83 period than in the 1983–89 period (1.6 percent versus 1.1 percent per year). Median wealth also grew much more slowly than mean wealth in the latter period (a difference of 0.8 percentage points per year). Overall, from 1983 to 1989, while mean wealth increased by 15 percent, median wealth grew by only 7 percent. The fact that mean wealth grew much faster than median wealth after 1983 implies that the bulk of the gains were concentrated at the top of the distribution—a finding that implies rising wealth inequality. The 1989–98 period was a repeat of the preceding one. While mean wealth grew by 11 percent, median wealth increased by only 4 percent.[5]

Rising Wealth Inequality in the 1980s

The rising level of wealth inequality between 1983 and 1989 is illustrated in Figure 3-3. The most telling finding is that the share of marketable net worth held by the top 1 percent, which had fallen 10 percentage points between 1945 and 1976, rose to 37 percent in 1989, compared with 34 percent in 1983. Meanwhile, the share of wealth held by the bottom 80 percent fell from 19 to 16 percent. Between 1989 and 1998, inequality continued to rise, though at a more moderate pace. The share of wealth held by the top 1 percent increased by another percentage point (to 38 percent), though the share of the bottom 80 percent stabilized.

These trends are mirrored in financial net worth, which is distributed even more unequally than total household wealth. In 1998, the top 1 percent of families as ranked by financial wealth owned 47 percent of the total (in contrast to 38 percent of total net worth). The top quintile accounted for 91 percent of total financial wealth, and the second quintile accounted for nearly all the remainder.

The concentration of financial wealth increased to the same degree as that of marketable wealth between 1983 and 1989. The

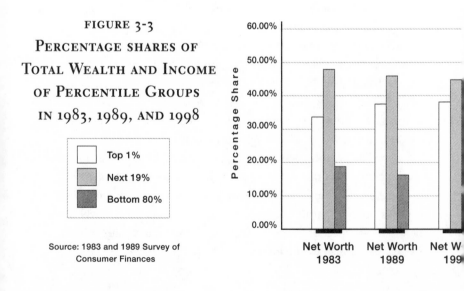

FIGURE 3-3

PERCENTAGE SHARES OF
TOTAL WEALTH AND INCOME
OF PERCENTILE GROUPS
IN 1983, 1989, AND 1998

Top 1%

Next 19%

Bottom 80%

Source: 1983 and 1989 Survey of
Consumer Finances

share of the top 1 percent of financial wealth holders increased by 4 percentage points, from 43 to 47 percent of total financial wealth. The share of the next 19 percent fell from 48 to 46 percent, while that of the bottom 80 percent declined from 9 to 7 percent. Between 1989 and 1998, the share of total financial wealth of the top 1 percent increased a bit more (by 0.4 percentage points) but the share of the bottom 80 percent recovered to where it was in 1983.

Income distribution, too, became more concentrated between 1983 and 1989. As with wealth, most of the relative income gain accrued to the top 1 percent of recipients, whose share of total household income grew by 4 percentage points, from 13 to 17 percent.[6] The share of the next 19 percent remained unchanged at 39 percent. Almost all the (relative) loss in income was sustained by the bottom 80 percent of the income distribution, whose share fell from 48 to 44 percent. Between 1989 and 1998, income inequality increased a bit more. While the share of the top 1 percent remained stable, the share of the next 19 percent rose by 0.6 percentage points and that of the bottom 80 percent correspondingly fell by 0.6 percentage points.

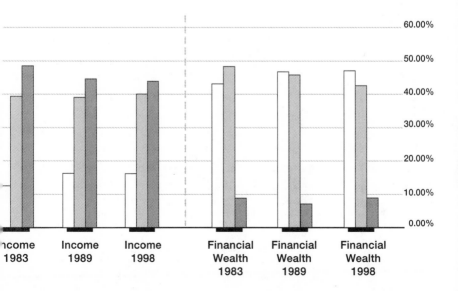

Another way to view rising wealth concentration is to look at how the increases in total wealth were divided over a specified period. This is calculated by dividing the increase in wealth of each group by the total increase in household wealth.[7] The results for 1983–98, shown in Figure 3-4, indicate that the top 1 percent of wealth holders received 53 percent of the total gain in marketable wealth over the period. The next 19 percent received 38 percent, while the bottom 80 percent received only 9 percent. This pattern represents a distinct turnaround from the 1962–83 period, when every group enjoyed some share of the overall wealth growth and the gains were roughly in proportion to the share of wealth held by each in 1962. Over this period, the top 1 percent received 34 per-

FIGURE 3-4

PERCENTAGE OF REAL WEALTH (INCOME) GROWTH
ACCRUING TO EACH PERCENTILE GROUP, 1983–1998

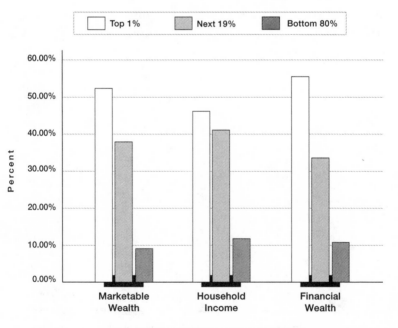

Source: 1983 and 1998 Survey of Consumer Finances

TABLE 3-1

NUMBER OF MILLIONAIRES AND
MULTIMILLIONAIRES, 1983–1998 IN 1,000S

YEAR	TOTAL NUMBER OF HOUSEHOLDS	NUMBER OF HOUSEHOLDS WITH NET WORTH EQUAL TO OR EXCEEDING[a]		
		$1,000,000	$5,000,000	$10,000,000
1983	83,893	2,411	247.0	66.5
1989	93,009	3,024	296.6	64.9
1992	95,462	3,104	277.4	41.6
1995	99,101	3,015	474.1	190.4
1998	102,547	4,783	755.5	239.4
PERCENT CHANGE:				
1983–1989	10.9%	25.4%	20.1%	-2.4%
1989–1998	10.3%	58.2%	154.7%	269.1%

a. 1998 dollars.

Source: 1983, 1989, 1992, 1995, and 1998 Survey of Consumer Finances,
Federal Reserve Board of Washington, D.C.

cent of the wealth gains, the next 19 percent claimed 48 percent, and the bottom 80 percent got 18 percent.

Gains in the overall growth in financial wealth were also distributed unevenly, with 56 percent of the growth accruing to the top 1 percent and 33 percent to the next 19 percent. The bottom 80 percent gained only 11 percent.

Finally, the changes in wealth distribution can be assessed by looking at the Gini coefficient. This indicator is used commonly to summarize data on the degree of inequality of income, wealth, or anything else of value. It ranges from 0 (exact equality) to 1 (one person owns everything); a higher Gini coefficient means greater inequality. This measure, like the others reviewed here, points to an increase in inequality: Between 1983 and 1989, the Gini coefficient increased from 0.80 to 0.84, between 1989 and 1998, the Gini coefficient remained at this high plateau.

The increase in wealth inequality recorded over the 1983–98 period—particularly between 1983 and 1989—in the United States is almost unprecedented. The only other period in the twentieth century during which concentration of household wealth rose comparably was from 1922 to 1929. Then, inequality was buoyed primarily by the excessive increase in stock values, which eventually crashed in 1929, leading to the Great Depression of the 1930s.

Despite the seemingly modest increase in overall wealth inequality during the 1990s, the decade witnessed a near explosion in the number of very rich households (see Table 3-1). The number of millionaires climbed by 54 percent between 1989 and 1998, the number of "pentamillionaires" ($5,000,000 or more) more than doubled, and the number of "decamillionaires" ($10,000,000 or more) almost quadrupled. Much of the growth occurred between 1995 and 1998 and was directly related to the surge in stock prices.

4

The Changing
Structure of
Household Wealth

In order to assess the likely incidence of wealth taxation in the United States—who is likely to pay and how much—it is necessary to analyze both the variation of household wealth by demographic group and the composition of wealth.

There are substantial differences in wealth holding by demographic category. Households headed by those aged 45–69[1] are by far the wealthiest in our country, with those 70 and over in second place and households headed by those under 45 a distant third. Between 1983 and 1998, the two less-privileged age cohorts made gains in relative wealth holdings. Over the same period, white and African-American households' mean wealth continued to converge. Nevertheless, the gap in mean wealth holdings between whites and blacks remained very large in comparison with income differences (a ratio of 0.18 for wealth versus 0.63 for income). The difference in median wealth between white and African-American households was even larger than that in mean wealth—a ratio of

FIGURE 4–1

RATIO OF MEAN MARKETABLE WEALTH TO THE
OVERALL MEAN BY AGE GROUP, 1962, 1983, 1989, AND 1998

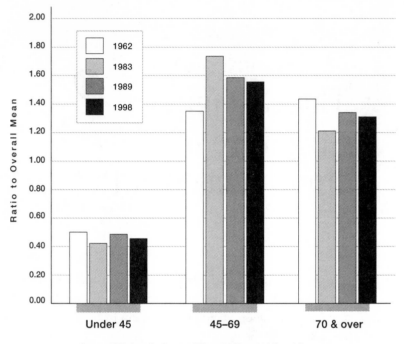

Source: 1962, from the Survey of Financial Characteristics of Consumers;
1983, 1989, and 1998, from the Survey of Consumer Finances

0.12—hinting that wealth inequality among blacks is greater than
that among the population at large.

WEALTH HOLDINGS BY AGE GROUP

One key predictor for differences in wealth among families is age.
Individuals typically accumulate wealth until retirement age; thereafter, they spend down their savings.[2] Figure 4-1 confirms this pattern. In 1998, the average marketable wealth of families whose
heads were under the age of 45 was far below the overall average,
while that of families with heads over 45 was well above the aver-

age, though less so in the case of elderly households. "Hump-shaped" profiles are also found for 1962, 1983, and 1989.

Despite the overall similarity in the three age-wealth profiles, there have been notable shifts in relative wealth holdings. Between 1962 and 1983, middle-aged households gained at the expense of both the younger and older households. The wealth of household-ers under age 45 declined from 50 percent of the average to 40 percent, that of the middle-aged group increased from 135 to 173 percent of the average, and that of the older group fell from 146 to 121 percent of the average.

The years 1983 to 1989 saw an exact reversal of this pattern. The wealth of families with heads under age 45 increased from 40 percent of the overall mean in 1983 to 49 percent in 1989, close to the corresponding 1962 figure. The relative wealth of the middle-aged fell from 173 percent of the average in 1983 to 158 in 1989, still above the comparable 1962 figure. The wealth holdings of older households grew from 121 percent in 1983 to 132 percent in 1989, remaining below their corresponding level in 1962. Between 1989 and 1998, there was not much change in the relative position of the two older age groups, but the wealth of families with heads under 45 fell back from 49 to 45 percent of the overall mean.[3]

RACIAL DIFFERENCES IN HOUSEHOLD WEALTH

On the basis of the Current Population Reports, the relative gap in income between African-American and white households was almost identical in 1967 and 1989 (see Table 4-1). The ratio of mean household income remained at 0.63, and the ratio of median income held at slightly below 0.6. The story of household wealth is more discouraging. From 1983 to 1989 the ratio of mean wealth fell (from 0.19 to 0.17), while the ratio of median wealth remained at the shockingly low level of 0.07. Between 1989 and 1998, things improved slightly. The ratio of mean wealth rose slightly (from 0.17 to 0.18) and the ratio of median wealth advanced from 0.07 to 0.12.[4]

Table 4-1

Ratio of Household Income, Wealth, and Homeownership Rates Between African-Americans and Whites, 1940–1998

	RATIO OF	
YEAR	MEANS	MEDIANS

I. Household Income[a]

1967	0.63	0.58
1970	0.65	0.61
1980	0.64	0.58
1983	0.62	0.57
1989	0.63	0.59
1998	0.63	0.62

a. The data source is the U.S. Bureau of the Census, "Detailed Historical Income and Poverty Tables from the March Current Population Survey, 1947–1998," available on the Internet at http://www.census.gov/-hhes/income/histinc/h04.html. Hispanic households may be classified in either group.

II. Homeownership Rate[b]

1940	0.52	
1950	0.61	
1960	0.60	
1970	0.64	
1980	0.65	
1983	0.65	
1989	0.65	
1998	0.67	

b. Calculations for 1940–1980 are based on decennial census data from the U.S. Bureau of the Census (1989), p. 70. Ratios for 1940–1970 are between whites and nonwhites. Hispanic households may be classified in either group. Figures for 1983–1998 are from the Survey of Consumer Finances and are between whites and African Americans only. Hispanics are excluded from these calculations.

III. Net Worth[c]

1962	0.12	0.04
1983	0.19	0.07
1989	0.17	0.07
1998	0.18	0.12

c. Figures for 1962 are from the Survey of Financial Characteristics of Consumers; for 1983, 1989, and 1998, from the Survey of Consumer Finances. Hispanics are excluded from these calculations.

Notably, the home ownership rate based on decennial census data almost doubled among nonwhite families between 1940 and 1980 (from 24 percent to 44 percent). Indeed, the ratio of home ownership rates between nonwhites and whites increased from 52 percent in 1940 to 64 percent in 1985. However, these increases were confined to the 1940s and the 1960s. In the 1950s and 1970s, there was no change. Between 1983 and 1989, according to the Survey of Consumer Finances (SCF) data, the home ownership rate among African-American families actually fell slightly, from 44 to 42 percent, but then rebounded to 46 percent in 1998. The ratio of home ownership rates between black and white families also increased slightly, from 65 percent in 1983 to 67 percent in 1998.

Turning to wealth more broadly defined, one finds that African-American families also made substantial gains on whites in terms of both mean and median net worth between the early 1960s and the early 1980s. According to the SCF data, the gap in both mean and median wealth remained unchanged during the 1980s but did close somewhat during the 1990s, particularly for median wealth. Still, in 1998, the gap in median wealth was quite a bit larger than in mean wealth. This result reflects a greater inequality in wealth among blacks than whites. In 1998, for example, 27 percent of black families reported zero or negative net worth, compared to 14 percent of whites. Thus, though there have been some gains in closing the racial wealth gap among better-off blacks, the differential remains large among less affluent families.

THE COMPOSITION OF WEALTH

The portfolio composition of household wealth shows the forms in which households save. Do households save for direct consumption, as in acquiring ownership of houses and automobiles? Do families save for precautionary reasons, as in the form of bank deposits? Do they save for retirement, as in insurance plans, IRAs (Individual Retirement Accounts), or the like? Or do they save mainly for investment purposes, as in financial securities and corporate stock?

Overall, between 1962 and 1989, there was a major corresponding shift in household portfolios from financial assets and equities
(deposits, bonds, stocks, and trusts), which declined from 52 percent
of gross wealth to 34 percent, to real estate and unincorporated
business equity, which rose from 48 percent to 64 percent. Debt as a
proportion of net worth, after falling from 16.4 to 15.1 percent
between 1962 and 1983, increased to 17.6 percent in 1989. Between
1989 and 1998, financial assets and equities rose from 34 to 42 percent of gross wealth, while real estate and business equity declined
from 64 to 58 percent. Debt as a fraction of net worth remained at
17.6 percent.

Many people believe that housing (more specifically, owner-occupied housing) is by far the most important asset the household controls. Owner-occupied housing was indeed the most important asset
in the household portfolio in 1962, 1983, 1989, and 1998 (see Figure
4-2). However, in none of the three years was its gross value more
than a third of total assets, or its net value more than one-quarter. In
1998, housing accounted for 29 percent of the gross value of assets,
and net equity in owner-occupied housing—the value of the house
minus any outstanding mortgage—was only 18 percent of gross
assets (or 22 percent of net worth). Checking deposits, savings
accounts (including money market funds), other deposits, and retirement plans (like IRAs)[5] amounted to 21 percent. Real estate other
than owner-occupied housing and unincorporated business equity
comprised 28 percent of total assets. Corporate stock, bonds, and
other financial securities, plus trust equity, amounted to 20 percent.
Debt as a proportion of gross assets was 15 percent.

There have been some significant changes in the composition of
household wealth since 1962. Popular perception is that housing is
the only substantial asset that most families can claim, but figures
show this is increasingly untrue. The gross value of housing as a
proportion of gross assets increased from 26 percent in 1962 to 30
percent in 1983, remained at this level in 1989, but then declined
slightly to 29 percent in 1998.[6] Other (nonhome) real estate and
business equity grew rapidly between 1962 and 1989, from 22 to 31

FIGURE 4-2

COMPOSITION OF HOUSEHOLD WEALTH
(PERCENT AF GROSS ASSETS)
1962, 1983, 1989, AND 1998

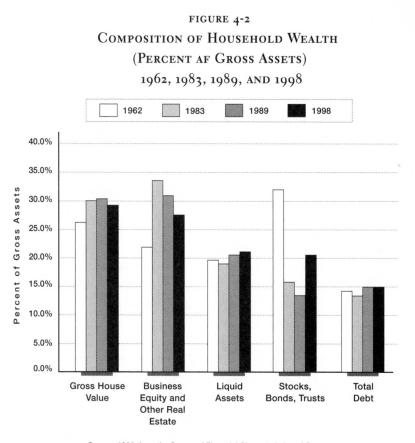

Source: 1962, from the Survey of Financial Characteristics of Consumers;
1983, 1989, and 1998, from the Survey of Consumer Finances

percent of total assets, but then declined to 28 percent in 1998. Liquid assets, including checking and savings accounts, money market funds, certificates of deposits (CDs), life insurance, and pension accounts, remained relatively steady at between 19 and 21 percent of total assets in 1962, 1983, 1989, and 1998. Financial securities (bonds), corporate stock, and trust equity declined in importance in the household portfolio from 32 percent in 1962 to 16 percent in 1983 and then to 13 percent in 1989; it then increased during the 1990s to 20 percent in 1998 (a reflection of the rapid increase in stock prices over the latter part of this decade).

DIFFERENCES IN WEALTH COMPOSITION

Figure 4-2 provides a picture of the average holdings of all families in the economy, but there are marked class differences in how middle-class families and the rich invest their wealth. As shown in Table 4-2, the richest 1 percent of households (as ranked by wealth) invested almost 80 percent of its savings in investment real estate, businesses, corporate stock, and financial securities in 1998. Corporate stocks, owned either directly by the households or indirectly through mutual funds, trust accounts, or various pension accounts, comprised 29 percent by themselves. Housing accounted for only 8 percent of household wealth, liquid assets another 5 percent, and pension accounts 7 percent. Their ratio of debt to net worth was 3 percent and their ratio of debt to income was 49 percent.

Among the next richest 19 percent of U.S. households, housing comprised 29 percent of their total assets, liquid assets another 11 percent, and pension assets 15 percent. Forty-three percent of their assets took the form of investment assets—real estate, business equity, stocks, and bonds—and 24 percent was in the form of stocks directly or indirectly owned. Debt amounted to 13 percent of their net worth and 90 percent of their income.

In contrast, about 60 percent of the wealth of the middle three quintiles (60 percent) of households was invested in owner-occupied housing in 1998. Another 24 percent went into monetary savings of one form or another and pension accounts. Together housing, liquid assets, and pension assets accounted for 84 percent of the total assets of the middle class. The remainder was split about evenly among nonhome real estate, business equity, and various financial securities and corporate stock. Stocks directly or indirectly owned amounted to only 11 percent of their total assets. The ratio of debt to net worth was 51 percent, much higher than that for the richest 20 percent, and their ratio of debt to income was 102 percent, also higher than the top quintile.

Another way to portray differences between middle-class households and the rich is to compute the share of total assets of differ-

TABLE 4-2

COMPOSITION OF WEALTH BY WEALTH CLASS, 1998
(PERCENT OF GROSS ASSETS)

CATEGORY	TOP 1 PERCENT[a]	NEXT 19 PERCENT[a]	MIDDLE 3 QUINTILES[a]
Principal residence	7.8	28.8	59.8
Liquid assets (bank deposits, money market funds, and cash surrender value of life insurance)	5.0	11.3	11.8
Pension accounts	6.9	14.9	12.3
Corporate stock, financial securities, mutual funds, and personal trusts	31.6	20.0	5.5
Unincorporated business equity, other real estate	46.9	23.2	8.8
Miscellaneous assets	1.8	1.8	1.8
Total assets	100.0	100.0	100.0
Debt/equity ratio	3.3	12.9	51.3
Debt/income ratio	49.4	90.2	101.6
All stocks/total assets[b]	28.7	24.1	11.2

a. Top 1 percent: Net worth of $3,352,100 or more.

   Next 19 percent: Net worth between $257,700 and $3,352,100.

   Quintiles 2 through 4: Net worth between $263 and $257,700.

b. Includes direct ownership of stock shares and indirect ownership through mutual funds, trusts, IRAs, Keogh plans, 401(k) plans, and other retirement accounts.

Source: 1998 Survey of Consumer Finances

TABLE 4-3
PERCENT OF TOTAL ASSETS HELD BY WEALTH CLASS, 1998

CATEGORY	TOP 1 PERCENT[a]	NEXT 9 PERCENT[a]	BOTTOM 90 PERCENT[a]	ALL	SHARE OF TOP 10% 1983	SHARE OF TOP 10% 1998
Stocks and mutual funds	49.4	35.7	14.9	100.0	90.4	85.1
Financial securities	50.8	33.2	15.9	100.0	82.9	84.1
Trusts	54.0	36.8	9.2	100.0	95.4	90.8
Business equity	67.7	24.0	8.3	100.0	89.9	91.7
Non-home real estate	35.8	39.1	25.1	100.0	76.3	74.9
Total for Group	54.1	32.1	13.8	100.0	85.6	86.2
Stocks, directly or indirectly owned[b]	42.1	36.6	21.3	100.0	89.7	78.7
Principal residence	9.0	26.2	64.8	100.0	34.2	35.2
Deposits[c]	19.5	31.5	49.0	100.0	52.9	51.0
Life insurance	11.3	41.5	47.2	100.0	33.6	52.8
Pension accounts[d]	19.7	40.2	40.2	100.0	67.5	59.8
Total for group	13.0	31.0	56.0	100.0	41.0	44.0
Total debt	7.1	19.9	73.0	100.0	31.8	27.0

a. Top 1 percent: Net worth of $3,352,100 or more.
Next 9 percent: Net worth between $475,600 and $3,352,100.
Bottom 90 percent: Net worth less than $475,600.

b. Includes direct ownership of stock shares and indirect ownership through mutual funds, trusts, and IRAs, Keogh plans, 401(k) plans, and other retirement accounts.

c. Includes demand deposits, savings deposits, time deposits, money market funds, and certificates of deposit.

d. IRAs, Keogh plans, 401(k) plans, the accumulated value of defined contribution pension plans, and other retirement accounts.

Source: 1983 and 1998 Survey of Consumer Finances, Federal Reserve Board of Washington D.C.

ent types held by each group (see Table 4-3). In 1998 the richest one percent of households held half of all outstanding stock, financial securities, and trust equity, two-thirds of business equity, and 36 percent of investment real estate. The top 10 percent of families as a group accounted for about 90 percent of stock shares, bonds, trusts, and business equity, and about three-quarters of nonhome real estate. Moreover, despite the fact that 48 percent of households owned stock shares either directly or indirectly through mutual funds, trusts, or various pension accounts, the richest 10 percent of households accounted for 79 percent of the total value of these stocks, only slightly less than its 85 percent share of directly owned stocks and mutual funds.

In contrast, owner-occupied housing, deposits, life insurance, and pension accounts were more evenly distributed among households. The bottom 90 percent of households accounted for about two-thirds of the value of owner-occupied housing, almost 50 percent of deposits and life insurance cash value, and 40 percent of the value of pension accounts. Debt was the most evenly distributed component of household wealth, with the bottom 90 percent of households responsible for 73 percent of total indebtedness.

There was relatively little change between 1983 and 1998 in the concentration of asset ownership, with three exceptions. First, the share of total stocks and mutual funds held by the richest 10 percent of households declined from 90 to 85 percent over this period, and their share of stocks directly or indirectly owned declined from 90 to 79 percent. Second, the proportion of total pension accounts held by the top 10 percent fell from 68 percent in 1983 to 51 percent in 1989, reflecting the growing use of IRAs by middle-income families, and then rebounded to 60 percent in 1998 after the introduction of 401(k) plans and their adoption by high-income earners. Third, the share of total debt held by the top 10 percent also fell from 32 to 27 percent.

WHO HAS A STAKE IN THE STOCK MARKET?

There have been numerous reports in the media that stock ownership has substantially widened in the United States, particularly during the 1990s. There is some truth to these reports. The proportion of households owning some stock either outright or indirectly through mutual funds, trusts, or various pension accounts increased from 24.4 percent in 1983 to 48.2 percent in 1998 (see Table 4-4). Much of the increase was fueled by the growth in pension accounts like IRAs, Keogh plans, and 401(k) plans. Indeed, between 1983 and 1989, direct stock ownership declined somewhat (from 13.7 to 13.1 percent)—likely a result of the 1987 stock market plunge. However, the share of households with pension accounts nearly doubled over this period, from 11 to 23 percent, accounting for the overall increase in stock ownership. Between 1989 and 1998, the direct ownership of stocks grew rather modestly, by 6 percentage points, while the share of households with a pension account again doubled, accounting for the bulk of the overall increase in stock ownership.

Despite the overall gains in stock ownership, less than half of all households had any stake in the stock market by 1998. Moreover, many of these families had only a minor stake. In 1998, while 48 percent of households owned some stock, only 36 percent had total stock holdings worth $5,000 or more and only 32 percent owned $10,000 or more of stock.

Stock ownership is also highly skewed by wealth and income class. As shown in Table 4-5, 93 percent of the very rich (the top 1 percent) reported owning stock either directly or indirectly in 1998, compared to 46 percent of the middle quintile and 19 percent of the poorest 20 percent. While over 91 percent of the very rich also reported stocks worth $10,000 or more, only 26 percent of the middle quintile and less than 2 percent of the bottom quintile did so. The top 1 percent of households owned 42 percent of all stocks, the top 5 percent two-thirds, the top 10 percent almost 80 percent, and the top quintile almost 90 percent.

Stock ownership also tails off by income class (see bottom panel

TABLE 4-4

PERCENT OF HOUSEHOLDS OWNING STOCK DIRECTLY OR
INDIRECTLY, 1983–1998

	1983	1989	1992	1995	1998
Any stock holdings	24.4	31.7	37.2	40.4	48.2
Stock worth $5,000 or more[a]	14.5	22.6	27.3	29.5	36.3
Stock worth $10,000 or more[a]	10.8	18.5	21.8	23.9	31.8

a. 1998 dollars.

Source: 1983, 1989, 1992, 1995, and 1998 Survey of Consumer Finances, Federal Reserve
Board of Washington, D.C. Figures include direct ownership of stock shares and indirect
ownership through mutual Funds, trusts, and IRAs, Keogh plans, 401(k) plans, and
other retirement accounts.

of Table 4-5). Whereas 93 percent of households in the top income
class (those who earned $250,000 or more) owned stock in 1998, 52
percent of the middle class (income between $25,000 and $50,000),
29 percent of the lower middle class (income between $15,000 and
$25,000), and only 11 percent of poor households (income under
$15,000) reported stock ownership. The comparable ownership fig-
ures for stock holdings of $10,000 or more are 92 percent for the
top 1 percent, 27 percent for the middle class, 13 percent for the
lower middle class, and 5 percent for the poor. Moreover, about
three-quarters of all stocks were owned by the top 16 percent of
households (those earning $75,000 or more) and 88 percent were
owned by the top third of households (by income).

Thus, in terms of wealth or income, substantial stock holdings
have still not penetrated much beyond the reach of the rich and the
upper middle class. The big winners from the stock market boom of
the last few years have been these groups, while the middle class
and the poor have not seen sizable benefits from the bull market. It
is also apparent, therefore, which groups benefit from the preferential tax treatment of capital gains.

TABLE 4-5
CONCENTRATION OF STOCK OWNERSHIP BY WEALTH AND INCOME CLASS, 1998

CATEGORY	PERCENT OF HOUSEHOLDS OWNING STOCK WORTH MORE THAN			PERCENT OF STOCK OWNED	
	$0	$4,999	$9,999	SHARES	CUMULATIVE
WEALTH CLASS					
Top 1 percent	93.2	92.9	91.2	42.1	42.1
Next 4 percent	89.0	87.0	86.1	25.0	67.2
Next 5 percent	83.9	80.4	78.9	10.6	77.7
Next 10 percent	78.7	74.0	71.6	11.1	88.8
Second quintile	58.9	49.8	45.4	7.7	96.5
Third quintile	45.8	32.7	25.9	2.6	99.1
Fourth quintile	35.1	15.1	8.6	0.7	99.8
Bottom quintile	18.6	4.6	1.8	0.2	100.0
All	48.2	36.3	31.8	100.0	
INCOME LEVEL					
$250,000 or more	93.3	92.7	91.9	36.1	36.1
$100,000–$249,999	89.0	85.5	82.8	27.7	63.9
$75,000–$99,999	80.7	70.4	66.5	10.8	74.7
$50,000–$74,999	70.9	55.6	48.8	13.1	87.8
$25,000–$49,999	52.0	34.3	27.4	8.5	96.3
$15,000–$24,999	29.2	16.9	12.9	2.6	98.9
Under $15,000	10.6	5.2	4.5	1.1	100.0
All	48.2	36.3	31.8	100.0	

Figures include direct ownership of stock shares and indirect ownership through mutual funds, trusts, IRAs, Keogh plans, 401(k) plans, and other retirement accounts.

Source: 1998 Survey of Consumer Finances, Federal Reserve Board of Washington, D.C.

5

Comparisons with Other Countries

Due to differences in reference sources, in definitions of household wealth, and in accounting conventions, international comparisons of household wealth inequality must be made cautiously. However, the evidence seems to suggest that in the early part of the twentieth century (the 1920s are the earliest period for which data are available), wealth inequality was much lower in the United States than in the United Kingdom, with U.S. figures more comparable to Sweden's. Indeed, America appeared to be the land of opportunity, whereas Europe was a place where an entrenched upper class controlled the bulk of wealth. By the early 1990s, however, the situation appeared to have completely reversed, with a much higher concentration of wealth in the United States than in Europe. Europe now appears to be the land of equality.

United Kingdom and Sweden. There are two other countries besides the United States for which long-term data are available on household wealth inequality: the United Kingdom and Sweden.

The most comprehensive data exist for the United Kingdom. These data are based on estate duty (tax) return data and, as a result, use mortality multipliers to obtain estimates of the wealth of the living (see Appendix for methodology). Estimates are for the adult population (that is, individuals, not households). Figures are available on an almost continuous basis from 1923 to 1991.[1]

The Swedish data are available on a rather intermittent basis from 1920 through 1992. The data are based on actual wealth tax returns. Tax return data are subject to error, like other sources of wealth data. The principal problem is underreporting owing to tax evasion and legal tax exemptions. However, some assets, such as housing and stock shares, are extremely well covered in Sweden because of legal registration requirements. Also, the deductibility of interest payments from taxable income makes it likely that the debt information is very reliable. On the other hand, bank accounts and bonds are not subject to similar tax controls, and it is likely that their amounts are underreported.

Figure 5-1 shows comparative trends among the three countries.[2] For the United Kingdom, there was a dramatic decline in the degree of individual wealth inequality from 1923 to 1974 but little change

FIGURE 5-1

SHARE OF MARKETABLE NET WORTH HELD BY TOP PERCENTILE OF WEALTHHOLDERS: SWEDEN, UNITED KINGDOM, UNITED STAES, 1920–1992

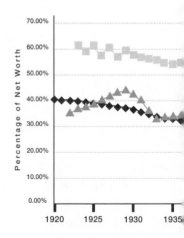

Source: Board Of Inland Revenue (United Kingdom).
Inland Revenue Statistics, 1993 (London: Her Majesty's
Statistical Office, 1993), Series C, Table 13.5.

thereafter. Based on a conventional definition of wealth (marketable wealth), the share of the top 1 percent of wealth holders fell from 61 percent in 1923 to 23 percent in 1974. However, between 1974 and 1991, there was only a relatively minor reduction in the concentration of household wealth, as the top percentile saw its share remain at 23 percent.

In Sweden, as in the United Kingdom, there was a dramatic reduction in wealth inequality between 1920 and the mid-1970s. Based on the years for which data are available, the decline appears to have been a continuous process. Over this period, the share of the top percentile declined from 40 percent to 17 percent of total household marketable wealth. Between 1975 and 1985, there was virtually no change in the concentration of wealth. However, this was followed by a sharp increase in wealth inequality between 1985 and 1992, with the share of the top percentile increasing to 20 percent, a level similar to that of the mid-1960s.

Comparisons among the three countries are instructive. In all three countries, there was a fairly sizable reduction in wealth concentration until the late 1970s, though the pattern was much more cyclical in the United States than in the other two. However, during

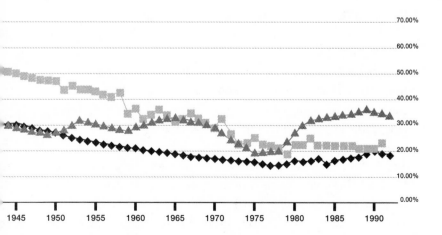

the 1980s, both the United States and Sweden showed a rather sharp increase in wealth inequality, whereas the trend was almost flat in the United Kingdom. This is a surprising difference, since both the United States (under Ronald Reagan) and the United Kingdom (under Margaret Thatcher) pursued conservative economic policies while the Social Democrats dominated in Sweden. Moreover, of the three countries, Sweden is the only one with a direct tax on household wealth. This suggests that differences in public policy alone cannot account for these trends in wealth distribution.

Other OECD Countries. Figures on the size distribution of household wealth for six OECD countries in the mid-1980s are shown in Table 5-1. The data are grouped by relatively comparable sources. Section A shows comparative figures on the size distribution of household gross wealth for France and the United States which are based on a special study to create conformable databases between the two countries.[3] For gross assets in France, the share of the top 1 percent is 26 percent of the total, and that of the top 5 percent is 43 percent; the overall Gini coefficient is 0.71. The shares of the top 1 and 5 percent are considerably higher in the United States than in France. On the basis of the original U.S. data adjusted to the French concept of wealth, the American Gini coefficient is 0.77, considerably higher (more unequal) than that of France.

The results indicate that wealth is more unequally distributed in the United States than in France. The differences are considerable. This result is also consistent with the finding that French households keep a substantially higher proportion of their wealth in the form of owner-occupied housing, which is more equally distributed among the population than most other assets (particularly bonds and corporate stock).[4]

Section B shows comparative statistics for Germany and the United States derived from another conformable database—the German Socio-Economic Panel (GSOEP) and the U.S. Panel Study of Income Dynamics (PSID) Equivalent Data File for 1988—

TABLE 5-1

INEQUALITY OF HOUSEHOLD WEALTH IN SELECTED
COUNTRIES, MID-1980S (DERIVED FROM SIMILAR
DATA SOURCES)

SOURCE	GINI COEFFICIENT	PERCENT OF TOTAL WEALTH HELD BY:	
		TOP 1%	TOP 5%
A. Conformable Databases, Gross Assets			
1. France, 1986	0.71	26	43
2. United States, 1983	0.77	33	54
B. Conformable Databases, Net Worth			
1. Germany, 1988	0.69		
2. United States, 1988	0.76		
C. Net Worth, Comparable Household Surveys			
1. United States, 1983	0.79	35	56
2. Canada, 1984	0.69	17	38
3. Japan, 1981	0.58		
4. Japan, 1984	0.52	25	
5. Sweden, 1985–86		16	31

Source: Wolff, (1996). See the paper for details on sources and methods.

which attempts to make the wealth concept used in the two databases consistent by including the same set of assets and liabilities.
Also, the sampling frames are relatively similar, since they are both
panel datasets based on representative samples. The results also
show that the United States is the more unequal of the two countries, with a Gini coefficient of 0.76 compared to 0.69 for
Germany.[5]

Section C shows wealth statistics derived from several comparable household surveys. The first of these is the United States' 1983

Survey of Consumer Finances and the second is the 1984 Statistics Canada Survey of Consumer Finances.[6] Wealth inequality is clearly greater in the United States, with a share of the top percentile almost double that of Canada's. Estimates for Japan are shown for 1981 and 1984, on the basis of Japan's 1981 Family Saving Survey and its 1984 National Survey of Family Income and Expenditure; figures for Sweden are from its 1985–86 survey, "Household Market and Non-market Activities."[7] The results suggest that wealth inequality is considerably lower in Japan and Sweden than in the United States.

Weighing the evidence leads to the judgment that wealth inequality in the United States is high by international standards. It appears to be higher than in France, Germany, Canada, and Japan, and, despite the differences in sources and methods, higher than in Sweden and the United Kingdom during the postwar period, particularly since 1980. This result is perhaps not too surprising, since many studies have shown that recent income inequality is greater as well in the United States than in most other industrialized economies.[8] Moreover, the fact that both income and wealth inequality have continued to increase in the United States in the 1990s and that income inequality, in particular, has risen faster in the United States in the 1990s than in other OECD countries[9] leads one to believe that the U.S. continues to remain today the most unequal country in terms of wealth.

6

Wealth Inequality versus Income Inequality

Wealth inequality is today and has always been extreme and substantially greater than income inequality. Indeed, the top 1 percent of wealth holders has typically held in excess of one-quarter of total household wealth, compared to the 8 or 9 percent share of income received by the top percentile of the income distribution. Figure 6-1 shows the historical pattern of wealth and income inequality based on the percent share held by the most prosperous families.[1]

Forty-seven percent of the total real income gain between 1983 and 1998 accrued to the top 1 percent of income recipients (in contrast to 53 percent of the marketable wealth gain), 42 percent went to the next 19 percent of the income distribution, and 12 percent accrued to the bottom 80 percent (versus only 9 percent of the marketable wealth gain). While not quite as powerfully as in the case of wealth, these results for income show again that the growth in the economy during the 1980s and 1990s was concentrated in a surprisingly small part of the population. To put it succinctly, the top quintile received a little less than 90 percent of the total increase in

FIGURE 6-1

WEALTH INEQUALITY VERSUS INCOME INEQUALITY
1922–1998

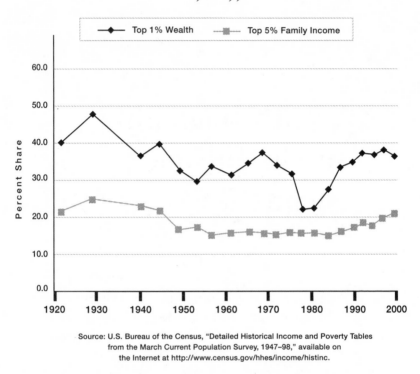

Source: U.S. Bureau of the Census, "Detailed Historical Income and Poverty Tables
from the March Current Population Survey, 1947–98," available on
the Internet at http://www.census.gov/hhes/income/histinc.

income and over 90 percent of the increase in wealth.[2] The stark-
ness of these numbers suggests a widening fissure separating the
strata within our society.

Though wealth is more unequally distributed, the historical
course of wealth distribution has roughly paralleled that of income
distribution. Income inequality, as measured by the share of income
flowing to the top 5 percent of income earners, increased between
1922 and 1929 from 21.2 to 25.1 percent, declined steadily during
the depression years—reaching a 21.8 percent share in 1939—and
then fell precipitously during World War II. There was a slight
decline between 1945 and 1953, but then income inequality
remained virtually flat until 1981. Between 1981 and 1989, it rose

fairly sharply, from 16.4 to 18.9 percent, and then surged to 21.4 percent in 1998, roughly the same level as in 1922.

The comparison of trends in income inequality and wealth inequality during the 1980s and 1990s is revealing, particularly since the former has received so much attention in both professional economic journals and the mass media. The evidence presented in Figure 6-1 indicates that the level of wealth concentration was at a postwar high in 1998. The time series on income inequality indicates exactly the same result for the concentration of household income. Moreover, the run-up in wealth inequality that characterized the 1980s had a twentieth-century precedent only during the 1920s. A similar finding can be reported for income inequality.

It is hard to provide a direct comparison of the degree of increase in inequality for the two series because of limitations on data availability. The Gini coefficient for wealth inequality shows an increase from 0.80 in 1983 to 0.84 in 1998. Based on the Census Bureau's Current Population Report series, the coefficient for income inequality rose from 0.41 to 0.46 over the same period.[3] The share of wealth held by the top 5 percent of wealth holders increased from 56 to 60 percent over these years, whereas the share of total income received by the top 5 percent of income recipients moved upward from 16.4 to 21.4 percent. The change in wealth inequality was more pronounced even if the years in question are 1977 to 1998, which includes the entire period of growing income inequality. Over this period, the Gini coefficient for income inequality increased by 0.05, and the income share of the top 5 percent increased by 5.3 percentage points.

It was reported earlier that the bottom two quintiles of wealth holders experienced an absolute decline in average net worth (in real terms) between 1983 and 1998. Were trends in real income comparable? According to the Current Population Report series, the mean income of each of the bottom two quintiles increased in real terms over the period (by 7 percent and 10 percent, compared to 38 percent for the top 5 percent of the distribution). However, it is striking that the average real incomes of both the bottom quintile and the

FIGURE 6-2

WEALTH INEQUALITY AND THE RATIO OF STOCK
TO HOUSING PRICES, 1922–1998

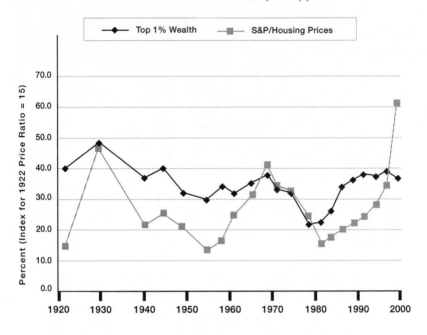

Sources: Standard and Poor 500 Composite Stock Index:
(1) From 1922 to 1969: U.S. Bureau of the Census, *Historical Statistics of the
United States, Colonial Times to 1970*, Bicentennial Edition, Part I, Washington,
D.C., U.S. Government Printing Office, 1975, p. 1004; (2) From 1970 to 1998: U.S.
Council of Economic Advisers, *Economic Report of the President, 2000*,
Washington, D.C., U.S. Government Printing Office, 2001, Table B-93, p. 406.
Median House Prices: House Prices (1) From 1922 to 1969: U.S. Bureau of the
Census, *Historical Statistics of the United States, Colonial Times to 1970*,
Bicentennial Edition, Part I, Washington, D.C., U.S. Government Printing Office,
1975, Series N 259 and 261, p. 647. (2) From 1970 to 1998: U.S. Bureau of the
Census, *Statistical Abstract of the United States, 1999*, 119th edition, Washington,
D.C., U.S. Government Printing Office, 1999, Table No. 1203, p. 725.

second-lowest were actually only slightly greater in 1998 than in
1973, even though overall mean income for the entire population
had grown over this period.[4] Thus, poorer households saw their net
worth decline at the same time that their incomes were stagnating.

It is apparent that the time patterns of wealth inequality and income inequality have been similar but not identical across the century. Income inequality was generally stable during the postwar years until 1981, while wealth inequality fell sharply during the 1970s. What can explain this discrepancy? One variable that appears to figure significantly in movements in wealth inequality is the ratio of stock prices to housing prices. Stocks are an asset held primarily by the upper classes, whereas housing is the major asset of the middle classes. If stock prices increase relative to housing prices, the share of wealth held by the top wealth groups will rise.[5]

The ratio of stock prices to housing prices (indexed to a value of 15 in 1922 in order to fit the curve onto Figure 6-2) shows a time graph similar to that of wealth inequality. The ratio more than trebled between 1922 and 1929, corresponding to a tremendous growth in wealth inequality. It fell by half between the 1929 crash and 1933 as wealth inequality also declined, and then it increased by about 20 percent between 1933 and 1939 as the stock market partially recovered, paralleling a new rise in wealth inequality. The price ratio then fell by almost half between 1939 and 1949 because of a rapid inflation in housing prices, which, in turn, was accompanied by a pronounced decline in wealth inequality.

The ratio of stock to housing prices more than trebled between 1949 and 1965, and this movement corresponded to a rise in wealth inequality. Between 1965 and 1979, the ratio fell by almost two-thirds, with most of the decline occurring after 1972. Before 1972, the main culprit was rising housing prices, but subsequently the principal reason was a stagnating stock market. This period was, not surprisingly, characterized by a dramatic decline in wealth inequality. Between 1979 and 1998, the price ratio almost quadrupled as the stock market flourished (particularly in the late 1990s), in line with the sharp increase in wealth inequality that was also recorded over this period.[6]

7

Current Systems of Wealth Taxation

Given both the high and rising degree of wealth inequality in the United States, it seems reasonable to consider the possibility of extending the tax base to include personal wealth holdings. Such a policy not only promotes greater equity in our society—particularly by targeting those who have a greater ability to pay—but it may also provide households with an incentive for switching from less productive (those with a low rate of return) to more productive forms of assets. This chapter summarizes the forms of wealth taxation currently in place in the United States and other industrialized countries as a prelude to an analysis of some of the potential effects of introducing direct wealth taxation.

THE UNITED STATES

Household wealth is currently taxed in two ways on the federal level in the United States: estate taxes and capital gains taxes. Federal estate taxes were first introduced in 1916, with major revisions in

1976 and 1981. Capital gains were originally included in the personal income tax system, introduced in 1913. Their provisions and corresponding taxes have been modified over time on a recurrent basis.[1]

Estate Taxes. The current system provides for the taxation of the value of an estate at the time of death of an individual. The tax is levied on the value of the estate left, in contrast to the value of an inheritance received (see page 47 for a discussion of the "inheritance tax"). Moreover, the estate tax system is integrated with the gift tax, which refers to the voluntary transfer of assets from one (living) individual to another. In principle, gifts are aggregated over the lifetime of the individual donor, and the lifetime aggregate of gifts is combined with the value of an estate at death. The estate tax applies to the full value of gifts and estates.[2]

As of February 2001, each individual is exempted from estate taxes on net worth up to $675,000. The basic exemption is scheduled to rise to $1,000,000 in 2006. Wealth above that amount is levied at marginal tax rates, which begin at 37 percent and reach as high as 55 percent (for estates over $3,675,000). The estates of fewer than 48,000 individuals—about 2 percent of annual deaths—are subject to the estate tax. About half the total is paid out of estates worth $5,000,000 or more—about 4,000 people. At the time of this writing, President George W. Bush has proposed the complete elimination of the estate tax.

All forms of wealth are included in the tax base for calculating the gift-estate tax except pension annuities and life insurance. Assets are appraised at market value at the time of death, though special rules apply to farm property, closely held business, and unquoted stock and shares. For gifts, the first $10,000 per recipient ($20,000 in the case of a married couple) are exempt from the combined gift-estate tax. There is also full exemption for transfers (both gifts and estates) between spouses. Though there is no statutory provision for indexing tax thresholds to inflation, threshold changes over time have more than compensated for price changes.

Several states also levy estate taxes, which are generally based on federal rules.

Capital Gains. Capital gains refer to the difference between the purchase price and selling price of an asset. There are some adjustments made for the value of capital improvements in the case of real property (such as a home); these are figured in on a cost basis when computing capital gains. In the United States, capital gains are taxed as part of the federal income tax system (and state income tax systems). Only realized capital gains are included (that is, capital gains on actual sales of assets).

As of 2001, capital gains on assets held more than five years are subject to a maximum tax of 18 percent (compared to the top marginal income tax rate of 39.6 percent). Short-term capital gains (held for less than five years) are treated as ordinary income and do not receive tax preference.[3] However, in the case of owner-occupied housing, there is no tax levied on capital gains in the case when a new primary residence is purchased whose price exceeds the selling price of the old home. There is also a one-time exclusion of $500,000 (for a married couple; $250,000 for an individual) in capital gains on the sale of a primary residence. The tax liability on capital gains on gifts is deferred until the asset is sold. Capital gains on assets that enter an estate at the time of death are exempt from taxation.

OTHER OECD COUNTRIES

Other member countries of the OECD have much more extensive taxation of household wealth.[4] Besides taxation of estates at death and of capital gains, many countries also impose direct taxation on household wealth.

Direct Wealth Taxation. As of 1990, eleven of the twenty-four OECD countries had systems in place with direct taxation of household wealth: Austria, Denmark, Finland, Germany, Luxembourg, the Netherlands, Norway, Spain, Sweden, and

Switzerland (see Table 7-1). In addition, France had such a system in place from 1982 to 1987 and Ireland from 1975 to 1977.[5] Also, with the exception of Spain, most of these systems have been in place for at least sixty years. In all eleven countries, the wealth tax is administered in conjunction with the personal income tax. In all cases except Germany, a joint tax return is filed for both income and wealth.

Though actual provisions vary among these eleven countries, the basic structure of the tax is very similar in each. The countries differ in terms of the level at which the wealth tax takes effect. The thresholds for married couples with two children range from a low of $9,000 in Luxembourg to a high of $155,000 in Denmark. In Germany, the threshold is $129,000; in the Netherlands, $51,000; and in France, it was (when the tax was in effect) $520,000. These threshold levels do not include the forms of wealth that are entirely excluded from the tax base (see page 54). Moreover, there are income exclusions in many countries, so that a joint income-wealth threshold must be passed in order for the wealth tax to become effective.

In several of the countries (such as Denmark, the Netherlands, and Sweden), there are also ceilings on the total amount payable in both income and wealth taxes combined. These ceilings are usually expressed as a percentage of taxable income (in the Netherlands, for example, it is 80 percent of taxable income).

Tax rates on household wealth tend to be quite low, on the order of a few percent at most. Five countries have a flat-rate system: Austria, 1.0 percent; Denmark, 2.2 percent; Germany, 0.5 percent; Luxembourg, 0.5 percent; and the Netherlands, 0.8 percent. The other countries have graduated marginal tax rates: Finland, 1.5 percent at the threshold, rising to 1.7 percent at $296,000; Norway, 0.2 to 1.3 percent, the latter at $47,000; Spain, 0.2 to 2.0 percent, the top rate at $7.1 million; Sweden, 1.5 percent initially, reaching 3.0 percent at $140,000; and Switzerland, 0.05 percent, rising to 0.30 percent at $334,000.[6]

The countries also vary in the forms of wealth that are included in the tax base. All the countries except Spain exempt household and personal effects. Most include the value of jewelry above a certain amount. All except Germany include the value of automobiles, and all include boats.

Several of the countries exempt savings accounts up to a certain level ($4,600 in Germany, for example). All exclude pension rights and pension-type annuities. Other forms of annuities are generally exempt. About half the countries exempt life insurance policies, while the other half include some portion of them in the tax base.

The value of owner-occupied housing is taxable in all eleven countries. However, in Austria and Finland, a small deduction is allowed, while in the Netherlands and Norway, housing is valued at only a small percentage of its actual market value. Other forms of wealth, including bonds, stocks and shares, and unincorporated businesses, are included in the tax base in all countries.[7]

Most of the countries require an annual reassessment of the total value of personal property. However, Austria, Germany, and Luxembourg reassess every three years and Switzerland every two years. In principle, all eleven countries with a wealth tax system base the valuation of assets on current market value. However, in practice, this procedure is not always easy to enforce. First, some assets are not traded in the open market and hence do not have a readily available market price (small businesses and unquoted shares, for example). Second, housing presents a particular problem, since the usual method, based on the sale of "similar" property, depends in large measure on the definition of the similar class. On the other hand, bonds, quoted shares and stocks, and bank accounts are rather straightforward in their valuation.

Most of the countries use an "asset basis" to value unincorporated businesses, defined as the sum of the value of the individual assets contained in the business. This would typically understate the true value of the business, since no additional value is given to goodwill. Austria, Finland, and the Netherlands use a market value basis (the value of the business if it were sold immediately). Switzerland uses a formula based on the capitalized value of the business's profits over time.

Whereas most of the countries base their valuation of real property on its open market value, Austria uses a formula based on changes in the average costs of construction and changes in land prices. Germany uses the assessed valuation for local taxes. Luxembourg uses a formula based on the capitalized rental value of property.

Death Taxes. Twenty-two of the twenty-four OECD countries have death or gift taxes, or both (see Table 7-1). The only exceptions are Australia and Canada. However, most of the OECD countries have "inheritance taxes" in lieu of the American-style estate tax. The difference between the two is that inheritance taxes are assessed on the recipient, whereas an estate tax is assessed on the estate left by the decedent. With an inheritance tax, the tax schedule is applied to each individual bequest, whereas with an estate tax, the assessment is on the total value of the transfer. The inheritance tax has certain advantages over the estate tax. First, it can be adjusted more closely to the ability of an heir to pay the tax. Second, preferential treatment can be accorded to immediate family as opposed to more distant relatives or friends (so-called consanguinity basis).[8]

Of the four countries with estate taxes—Italy, New Zealand, the United Kingdom, and the United States—the amount exempted from tax varies from $20,000 for Italy to $675,000 for the United States (in 2001). Marginal tax rates range from 3 to 31 percent in Italy, 30 to 60 percent in the United Kingdom, and 37 to 55 percent in the United States. In New Zealand there is a flat rate of 40 percent. Spousal transfers are totally exempt in the United Kingdom and the United States but are taxed, with special treatment, in the other two countries. All four countries also have gift taxes. In Italy and the United States, these are aggregated over the giver's lifetime and combined with the estate at death to determine the taxable base for the estate tax.

The structure of inheritance taxes is more complicated. Marginal tax rates vary with the relationship of the heir to the decedent, as do

TABLE 7-1

WEALTH TAXATION SYSTEMS AMONG OECD COUNTRIES
ON INDIVIDUAL OR FAMILY WEALTH HOLDINGS

	DIRECT WEALTH TAXATION	TRANSFER TAX AT DEATH AND ON GIFTS	CAPITAL GAINS TAXATION	WEALTH, DEATH, AND GIFT TAX RECEIPTS AS PERCENTAGE OF TOTAL TAX REVENUE[a]
Australia	No	None	Income	0.01
Austria	Yes	Inheritance	None	0.51
Belgium	No	Inheritance	None	0.58
Canada	No	None	Income	0.03
Denmark	Yes	Inheritance	Separate	0.92
Finland	Yes	Inheritance	Income	0.50
France	1982–87	Inheritance	Income	0.85
Germany	Yes	Inheritance	None	0.42
Greece	No	Inheritance	None	0.94
Iceland	Yes	Inheritance	Income	—
Ireland	1975–77	Inheritance	Separate	0.30
Italy	No	Estate/ Inheritance	None	0.23
Japan	No	Inheritance	Income	1.19
Luxembourg	Yes	Inheritance	Income	0.51
Netherlands	Yes	Inheritance	None	0.94
New Zealand	No	Estate	None	0.19
Norway	Yes	Inheritance	Income	0.61
Portugal	No	Inheritance	None	0.83
Spain	Yes	Inheritance	Income	0.49
Sweden	Yes	Inheritance	Income	0.68
Switzerland	Yes	Estate/ Inheritance	Income	3.06
Turkey	No	Inheritance	Income	0.19
United Kingdom	No	Estate	None	0.64
United States	No	Estate	Income	0.77

a. Figures are for 1985.

Source: Organization for Economic Cooperation and Development (1985).

the tax thresholds. In France, for example, the amount exempted from tax for bequests to spouses is $40,000, and the marginal tax rates vary from 5 to 40 percent, whereas bequests to nonrelatives have a threshold of $1,500 with a flat rate of 60 percent applied to the transfer. All nineteen OECD countries with an inheritance tax also have an associated gift tax.

Capital Gains Taxation. Fifteen of the twenty-four OECD countries also provide for a tax on capital gains (see Table 7-1). All fifteen tax capital gains as they are realized (that is, at the time of sale). In thirteen of the fifteen countries, capital gains are included as part of the personal income tax, whereas in the other two (Denmark and Ireland), a separate tax is collected. Interestingly, in eight countries—Denmark, Finland, Iceland, Luxembourg, Norway, Spain, Sweden, and Switzerland—there is both a direct wealth tax and a tax on capital gains.

There is wide latitude in the tax treatment of these gains across countries. In the United States, long-term capital gains currently (as of 2001) receive tax preference, with a maximum tax rate of 18 percent. Short-term gains are treated as ordinary income. In Denmark, there is a flat rate of 50 percent, while in Switzerland, marginal rates range from 10 to 40 percent. In both cases, there is no separate treatment of short-term gains.

In Australia, Norway (with some exceptions), and Spain, both short-term and long-term gains are treated as ordinary income and taxed in accordance with the personal income tax schedule. In Canada, three-quarters of capital gains are included as ordinary income. In Japan, half of long-term capital gains are taxed as ordinary income, while short-term gains are treated as ordinary income. In Sweden, a proportion of long-term gains are taxed as ordinary income, with the proportion depending on the nature of the property and the period held, while short-term gains are treated as ordinary income.

In most countries with capital gains taxes, gains on principal residences are exempt from taxation. Exceptions are Switzerland, where such gains are fully taxable; Japan, where the first $178,000 of gains are exempt; Spain, where exemption is subject to the purchase of a new residence; and Sweden and the United States, where only the excess of the sale price over the purchase price of a new residence is subject to taxation.

Revenue Collection. Though on the books these wealth taxation mechanisms appear to be a formidable way of collecting revenue, in fact, such levies account for only a very small part of total tax revenue in the various OECD countries. The last column of Table 7-1 summarizes the total tax collections from direct wealth and estate/gift taxes as a percent of total government revenue in 1985. Unfortunately, these totals do not include the capital gains tax since it is very hard to break out from regular income tax receipts. Among the twenty-three countries shown, the average percent collected is only 0.67. The shares range from a low of 0.01 percent in Australia to a high of 3.06 percent in Switzerland. Switzerland is, moreover, the only country in which the direct wealth tax collects more than one percent of total tax revenue—2.25 percent in 1985. The United States is slightly above average, with 0.77 percent of its total tax revenue coming from estate and gift taxes (of which 0.74 is from estate taxes and 0.03 from gift taxes). In terms of the receipts from estate and gift taxes as a share of the total personal tax intake, the United States ranks fifth among OECD countries, after Japan, Greece, Portugal, and Switzerland. In 1998, total federal tax collections from estate and gift taxes in the United States amounted to $24.0 billion, or 1.4 percent of total tax revenues.[9]

One may wonder why these wealth taxes collect so little revenue, particularly when some of them have been in place for more than seventy years—plenty of time for refinement of their efficacy. Three possible reasons suggest themselves. First, particularly in Europe, tax proceeds from the personal income tax and the value-added tax on consumption are already quite substantial, so that, relative to total tax revenues, wealth tax collections appear small. This is particularly germane to countries such as Sweden that have a cap on combined income and wealth taxes. Second, there is the strong possibility of evasion or unintentional omissions. Unlike labor earnings and interest and dividend payments, which can be recorded at their source, it is much more difficult for a tax collection agency to obtain independent information on the financial securities, stock holdings, unquoted shares, or value of a family business owned by a household. Though real property must be registered with local tax authorities, there is still a possibility that its value will be underestimated for tax purposes.

A third and related reason is that it is easy to transfer financial wealth holdings across borders. With the exception of real property and most small businesses, a family normally can purchase assets outside the country of residence with ease. A country that imposes an excessive wealth tax may induce substantial capital flight. As a result, most countries with a wealth tax try to keep it more or less in line with that of other countries.

8

Simulations of Direct Wealth Taxation in the United States

This chapter provides simulation results of the potential revenue effects of three alternative wealth taxation systems as applied to U.S. household economic data. These are based on the actual tax codes of Germany, Sweden, and Switzerland. The distinctive characteristics of each plan are shown in Table 8-1.[1]

The first set of simulations was performed on the basis of the 1989 U.S. personal income tax schedules and the 1989 Survey of Consumer Finances.[2] While the data are not perfect, the results are encouraging.[3] Even a very modest wealth tax (like the Swiss system, with marginal tax rates ranging from 0.05 percent to 0.30 percent and an exclusion of about $50,000 in wealth) could have raised $38 billion in 1989. Moreover, in the process, only 3 percent of families would have seen their federal tax bill rise by more than 10 percent.

Simulations of alternative schemes for wealth taxation also suggest that a combined income-wealth taxation system may indeed be more equitable than our current income tax system. The wealth tax is, not surprisingly, progressive with respect to wealth. Its incidence would also fall more heavily on older households than on younger ones (older households tend to be wealthier), on married couples than on singles (the former are also richer, on average), and on white individuals than on nonwhites (white families are generally much wealthier). Although this approach does not take into account behavioral responses of families to the imposition of a wealth tax, the calculations can nonetheless give some guidance as to the overall magnitude of likely revenues and redistributional effects.

There are three questions of interest. First, how much additional tax revenue will be raised under each alternative wealth taxation scheme (revenue effects)? Second, which groups will likely bear the burden of the new taxation of wealth (incidence effects)? Third, how will the alternative wealth tax systems affect overall inequality in the population and within different demographic groups (distributional effects)?

Revenue Effects

The actual U.S. personal income tax produces revenues of $445.7 billion, or 11.4 percent of total family income (details are tabulated in Table 8-2). A wealth tax following the German system would have produced total additional tax revenues of $67.5 billion in 1989, or 1.7 percent of total income. Adopting the German-style wealth tax would have increased tax revenues by 15 percent overall. Imposing the Swedish wealth tax, in contrast, would have added an additional $328.7 billion of personal taxes, amounting to 8.4 percent of total income and increasing the total tax intake by 74 percent. The Swiss wealth tax would have raised $38.0 billion in taxes, representing 0.9 percent of total income and 8 percent of the total income tax proceeds. The Swedish wealth tax would thus have a massive effect on total tax revenues, while the other two would have moderate effects. However, even the German- and Swiss-style wealth taxes would yield new revenues considerably in excess of the actual collections from the estate and gift taxes, $8.7 billion in 1989.[4]

TABLE 8-1

DETAILS OF DIRECT WEALTH TAXATION SYSTEMS OF GERMANY, SWEDEN, AND SWITZERLAND

	GERMANY	SWEDEN	SWITZERLAND
A. THRESHOLDS			
1. Single persons	$33,000	$56,000	$34,000
2. Married couple, no children	$57,000	$56,000	$56,000
3. Married couple, two children	$129,000	$56,000	$56,000
B. TAX RATE SCHEDULES	Flat rate of 0.5 %	1.5% (to $28,000) 2.0% (next $28,000) 2.5% (next $140,000) 3.0% (over $196,000)	0.05% (to $83,000) 0.10% (next $139,000) 0.15% (next $225,000) 0.20% (next $333,000) 0.25% (next $333,000) 0.30% (over $1,113,000)
C. EXCLUSIONS	Household effects Automobiles Savings (up to $4,600) Pensions/annuities Life insurance (up to $4,600) Unincorporated business (up to $58,000; excess taxed at 75%)	Household effects Pensions/annuities Life insurance	Household effects Pensions/annuities
D. CEILING	None	75 percent up to $50,000 of taxable income; 80 percent on excess.	None

Source: Organization for Economic Cooperation and Development (1985).

INCIDENCE

The incidence of wealth taxes depends on the joint distribution of income and wealth. If the two were perfectly correlated, then everyone would experience a similar proportional increase in taxes (depending on the wealth tax schedule). However, income and wealth are far from perfectly correlated. There are certain groups, such as the elderly, that have large wealth holdings but relatively little income. On the other hand, some young households may have high earnings but relatively little wealth accumulation (the "yuppies"). This new tax may thus shift the burden away from young households onto elderly ones.

Table 8-2 shows estimates of the new effective tax rates for U.S. taxpayers by income class, wealth class, age group, family type, and race.[5] The Swedish wealth tax system, like the graduated income tax in this country, is highly progressive with respect to income, rising from zero for the lowest income class to 15.7 percent for the highest. Moreover, the proportionate increase in total taxes paid is somewhat higher for upper-income families than for lower-income ones. In contrast, both the German and Swiss wealth tax systems tend to lay claim to an almost constant percentage of income, except for the highest income class, which pays a greater share with respect to its earnings. Moreover, in both cases, lower-income families' total tax bill rises proportionately more than higher-income families. While this may appear unfair, one must remember that the tax does not fall uniformly on lower-income families. Only a household with much wealth, regardless of income, is liable for taxation. Any household with substantial net worth may legitimately be viewed as capable of contributing to the public good.

The American income tax system is also progressive with respect to household wealth, with tax rates on income rising from 7.2 percent for the lowest wealth class (under $25,000) to 17.2 percent for the richest ($1,000,000 or more). All three European wealth tax systems, not surprisingly, are also progressive with respect to wealth. Tax rates measured as a percentage of income would rise from zero for the lowest wealth class to 5.7 percent for the highest under the German tax system; from zero to 25.5 percent under the Swedish system; and from zero to 3.2 percent under the Swiss system. The proportionate increase in taxes would also be greater for wealthier families than poorer ones under all three systems.

Refer again to Table 8-2. Income tax rates in the United States show relatively little variation across age groups, rising from 9.2 percent for the youngest families to 12.3 percent for those aged 35–54, then falling back a bit for older cohorts. In contrast, under all three wealth tax systems, tax rates on U.S. income would rise monotonically with age group, reflecting the fact that wealth-income ratios increase with age. Under the German system, tax rates would range from 0.5 to 4.1 percent; under the Swedish system, from 2.3 to 16.9 percent; and under the Swiss system, from 0.3 to 1.9 percent. Under all three systems, taxes would increase proportionately more for older Americans than for younger ones.

There is also relatively little variation in U.S. income tax rates by family type. Unmarried males face the highest average income tax rates (12.3 percent), followed by married couples (11.7 percent) and single females (8.9 percent). Under all three wealth tax systems, married couples would face the highest tax rates, with unmarried male and female households taxed almost identically. Under the German system, married couples would pay 1.8 percent of income in wealth taxes, compared to 1.5 percent for unmarried males or females; in the Swedish system, the respective rates are 9.3 and 5.9 percent, and in the Swiss system, 1.0 and 0.7 percent.

White families generally pay higher tax rates than nonwhites— 11.9 percent compared to 8.7 percent—reflecting the higher relative incomes of whites. Under all three wealth tax systems, white families, on average far better endowed than minority families, would pay considerably higher taxes than nonwhites. Also, in all three cases, white families would see their tax bill rise proportionately more than nonwhite families.

DISTRIBUTIONAL EFFECTS

One can measure the effect of wealth taxation on inequality in three steps. First, figure out the inequality (based on the Gini coefficient) in the distribution of pretax income. Second, calculate the Gini coefficient of after-tax income resulting only from the imposition of the personal income tax. Third, compute the same measure for after-tax income resulting from both the income tax and each of the wealth tax systems. The distributional effect of the wealth tax will depend on its progressivity with respect to income, its magnitude, and the proportionate increase in taxes it generates by income class.

Results are shown in section A of Table 8-3. Among all U.S. families, the Gini coefficient for pretax income was 0.52 in 1989. The Gini coefficient for income after income taxes was 0.50, indicating that the personal income tax system has a modest equalizing effect on income distribution. Adding the Swedish wealth tax to the personal taxation formula results in a further reduction of the Gini coefficient to 0.48. The Swedish wealth tax thus has an equalizing effect on the income distribution similar in magnitude to the personal income tax system. However, neither the German nor the Swiss wealth tax has much effect on measured income inequality, mainly because of the small amount of revenue that they generate and their lack of progressivity with respect to income.

The distributional effect of the wealth tax systems does show some variation by age group, family type, and race. The equalizing effects of the wealth tax exert greater influence within older age groups than among younger ones. For the group age 70 and over, the imposition of the Swedish wealth tax system causes the Gini coefficient to fall from 0.54 to 0.49. The effects are stronger among married couples than unmarried individuals: Among married couples, the Gini coefficient declines from 0.45 to 0.42 when Swedish wealth taxes are added to income taxes. The equalizing effect is also larger among white families than among nonwhite ones.

Section B of Table 8-3 shows the same set of computations for

Table 8-2
Original Income Tax and New Wealth Taxes As a Percent of Family Income Based on Alternative Wealth Taxation Systems, 1989 (By Income Class, Wealth Class, Age Group, Family Type and Race)

	ORIGINAL U.S. INCOME TAX RATE	GERMAN WEALTH TAX	
		PERCENT OF INCOME	RATIO TO INCOME TAX
ALL FAMILIES	11.4	1.7	0.15
A. INCOME CLASS			
Under $5,000	0.0	1.3	—
$5,000–$9,999	1.1	0.9	0.76
$10,000–$14,999	3.1	1.1	0.35
$15,000–$24,999	5.2	1.4	0.27
$25,000–$49,999	8.0	1.1	0.13
$50,000–$74,999	11.2	0.9	0.08
$75,000–$99,999	13.5	1.7	0.13
$100,000 & over	17.1	3.0	0.18
B. WEALTH CLASS			
Under $25,000	7.2	0.0	0.00
$25,000–$49,999	8.3	0.0	0.00
$50,000–$74,999	9.2	0.1	0.02
$75,000–$99,999	9.4	0.3	0.03
$100,000–$249,999	10.8	0.7	0.07
$250,000–$499,999	12.9	1.8	0.14
$500,000–$999,999	14.4	3.1	0.22
$1,000,000 & over	17.2	5.7	0.33
C. AGE CLASS			
Under 35	9.2	0.5	0.05
35–54	12.3	1.2	0.09
55–69	11.9	3.2	0.27
70 and over	10.5	4.1	0.39
D. HOUSEHOLD TYPE			
Married Couple	11.7	1.8	0.15
Males, Unmarried	12.3	1.5	0.12
Females, Unmarried	8.9	1.5	0.17
E. RACE			
White	11.9	1.9	0.16
Nonwhite	8.7	0.9	0.10

Source: Author's calculations from the 1989 Survey of Consumer Finances.
See text for details on tax calculations.

| SWEDISH WEALTH TAX | | SWISS WEALTH TAX | |
PERCENT OF INCOME	RATIO TO INCOME TAX	PERCENT OF INCOME	RATIO TO INCOME TAX
8.4	0.74	0.9	0.08
0.0	—	0.6	—
0.7	0.57	0.3	0.27
2.3	0.75	0.5	0.15
4.2	0.82	0.7	0.13
5.0	0.62	0.5	0.06
5.0	0.45	0.4	0.04
8.8	0.66	0.8	0.06
15.7	0.92	1.7	0.10
0.0	0.00	0.0	0.00
0.0	0.00	0.0	0.00
0.4	0.05	0.2	0.02
1.4	0.15	0.5	0.05
4.2	0.39	0.4	0.04
10.3	0.80	0.4	0.03
17.8	1.24	1.0	0.07
25.5	1.48	3.2	0.19
2.3	0.25	0.3	0.03
6.6	0.54	0.6	0.05
14.6	1.22	1.5	0.13
16.9	1.60	1.9	0.18
9.3	0.79	1.0	0.08
5.9	0.48	0.7	0.05
5.9	0.66	0.6	0.06
9.2	0.77	0.9	0.08
3.9	0.44	0.5	0.05

an alternate measure of income called Income*. Income* is defined as family income plus 3.28 percent of family net worth (3.28 percent is an estimate of the average annual real rate of appreciation on household wealth over the 1962–89 period). Income* is logically a more inclusive measure of family welfare than normal income. The effects of a wealth tax on this more inclusive measure of income may be considered a better measure of the overall distributional effects of a wealth tax.

Results for Income* are quite similar to those for standard family income. Among all families, the Gini coefficient is 0.544 for pretax Income*, 0.527 for Income* after the payment of income taxes, and 0.502 for Income* after both income and Swedish wealth taxes are paid. As before, the German and Swiss wealth tax systems have little distributional impact. The equalizing effects of wealth taxes on the distribution of Income* increase with age, are greater for married couples than for singles, and are stronger among white than nonwhite families.

UPDATE TO 1998

These tax simulations were updated to 1998 on the basis of the 1998 Survey of Consumer Finances (SCF) and the 1998 income tax schedules for individuals. One advantage of the 1998 SCF data is that they provide information on household Adjusted Gross Income (AGI). Using this instead of the estimated value of AGI provides a better match of actual personal income taxes paid by families. The simulated value is only 7 percent above the actual personal income tax collections of $737.7 billion.[6]

In this analysis, only the Swiss wealth tax system has been used since it seems to provide the most reasonable amount of revenue generated. Following the Swiss convention, thresholds and tax brackets are indexed to consumer price changes. Using the CPI index for the United States, the new exemptions in 1998 are $83,000 for married couples and $51,000 for singles. The top bracket (the 0.30 percent range) now begins at $1.66 million.

The Swiss style wealth tax would have created $52 billion in extra tax revenue in 1998. This represents 1.0 percent of total family income and 7.1 percent of the total income tax revenue (see Table 8-4). This compares with actual U.S. personal income tax proceeds of $737.5 billion in 1998, or 13.8 percent of total income. It also contrasts with total estate and gift taxes of $24.1 billion in 1998. While 41 percent of families in 1998 would pay some additional wealth tax, only 16.7 percent of families would see their tax bill rise by more than $100 and only 8.5 percent by more than $300.

As in the 1989 simulations, the Swiss wealth tax system is progressive with respect to income, rising from 0.4 percent for the lowest income class to 1.9 percent for the highest bracket. However, now the percent increase in total taxes paid would also be higher for upper-income families than for lower-income ones. Moreover, the fraction of families paying any wealth tax would rise with income level, from 21 percent for the lowest income bracket (under $15,000 of income) to virtually 100 percent for the highest income class ($250,000 of income and over). The wealth tax is again highly progressive with respect to wealth. The only groups that would pay an additional 1 percent or more of income in federal taxes are the millionaires. Upper-wealth families would also see a higher proportionate increase in total federal taxes paid. Very few families (only 9 percent) worth less than $100,000 in net wealth would pay any wealth taxes, whereas virtually all families above this amount would wind up paying some wealth tax.

In terms of wealth tax incidence by demographic characteristic, the wealth tax would fall more heavily on older households than younger ones. Wealth tax rates on income would rise monotonically with age group, from 0.2 percent for the youngest age group (age 34 and under) to 1.5 percent for the oldest (age 70 and over), and wealth taxes as a percent of income taxes would also increase with age, from 1 percent for the youngest age group to 18 percent for the oldest. The share of families paying a wealth tax would likewise rise with age, from 12 percent for the youngest to 69 percent for the oldest age group.

TABLE 8-3
DISTRIBUTIONAL EFFECTS OF ALTERNATIVE WEALTH TAXATION
SYSTEMS, 1989 (BY AGE GROUP, FAMILY TYPE, AND RACE)

	AGE GROUP				
	ALL	18–34	35–54	55–69	70+
A. GINI COEFFICIENTS FOR INCOME					
Pretax Income	0.521	0.441	0.477	0.568	0.568
Original Post-tax Income	0.497	0.420	0.454	0.543	0.539
New Postincome/ German Wealth Tax	0.495	0.421	0.451	0.537	0.534
New Postincome/ Swedish Wealth Tax	0.476	0.414	0.434	0.505	0.487
New Postincome/ Swiss Wealth Tax	0.495	0.420	0.452	0.539	0.536
B. GINI COEFFICIENTS FOR INCOME*a					
Pretax Income*	0.544	0.453	0.499	0.599	0.603
Original Post-tax Income*	0.527	0.435	0.482	0.583	0.586
New Postincome*/ German Wealth Tax	0.522	0.433	0.478	0.577	0.578
New Postincome*/ Swedish Wealth Tax	0.502	0.426	0.460	0.550	0.548
New Postincome*/ Swiss Wealth Tax	0.524	0.434	0.480	0.580	0.582

a. Income* is defined as family income plus 3.28 percent of family net worth.

Source: Author's calculations from the 1989 Survey of Consumer Finances, Federal Reserve Board of Washington, D.C. See text for details on tax calculations.

FAMILY TYPE			RACE	
MARRIED COUPLE	UNMARRIED MALE	UNMARRIED FEMALE	WHITE	NON-WHITE
0.473	0.529	0.451	0.504	0.525
0.446	0.502	0.426	0.479	0.503
0.442	0.501	0.424	0.477	0.503
0.421	0.487	0.415	0.458	0.490
0.444	0.502	0.425	0.477	0.503
0.500	0.549	0.468	0.526	0.542
0.481	0.528	0.449	0.509	0.524
0.475	0.524	0.445	0.504	0.521
0.453	0.509	0.430	0.483	0.510
0.478	0.526	0.447	0.506	0.522

TABLE 8-4

ORIGINAL INCOME TAX AND NEW WEALTH TAXES MODELED AFTER THE SWISS SYSTEM, 1998 (BY INCOME CLASS, WEALTH CLASS, AGE GROUP, FAMILY TYPE, AND RACE)

	RATIO OF ORIGINAL U.S. INCOME TAX TO FAMILY INCOME
ALL FAMILIES	13.8
A. INCOME CLASS	
Under $15,000	19.4
$15,000–$24,999	1.1
$25,000–$49,999	7.0
$50,000–$74,999	9.8
$75,000–$99,999	12.4
$100,000–$249,999	15.6
$250,000 & over	26.4
B. WEALTH CLASS	
Under $100,000	9.1
$100,000–$249,999	9.0
$250,000–$499,999	11.6
$500,000–$749,999	13.7
$750,000–$999,999	15.1
$1,000,000–$2,499,999	21.7
$2,500,000 & over	27.2
C. AGE CLASS	
Under 35	15.4
35–54	13.0
55–69	16.3
70 and over	8.7
D. HOUSEHOLD TYPE	
Married Couple	15.4
Males, Unmarried	12.5
Females, Unmarried	5.5
E. RACE OR ETHNICITY	
White	14.8
African American	6.8
Hispanic	4.7
Other	11.5

Source: Author's calculations from the 1989 Survey of Consumer Finances. See text for details on tax calculations.

SWISS WEALTH TAX		PERCENT OF FAMILIES
PERCENT OF INCOME	RATIO TO INCOME TAX	PAYING WEALTH TAX
1.0	0.07	40.9
0.4	0.02	21.0
0.3	0.05	33.1
0.2	0.03	36.2
0.3	0.03	50.5
0.3	0.02	59.2
0.9	0.06	81.7
1.9	0.07	99.5
0.0	0.00	9.0
0.1	0.01	81.7
0.2	0.02	95.1
0.5	0.03	99.1
0.8	0.05	98.8
1.0	0.05	99.9
3.5	0.13	100.0
0.2	0.01	11.6
0.5	0.04	39.2
1.2	0.07	57.6
1.5	0.18	69.3
0.8	0.05	46.9
0.6	0.05	31.2
0.6	0.10	36.7
0.8	0.05	47.1
0.1	0.01	17.3
0.2	0.05	15.8
0.6	0.05	34.4

Under the Swiss wealth tax system, married couples would face a slightly higher tax rate than unmarried male and female households, which would be taxed almost identically. A somewhat higher percentage of married couples (47 percent) would pay any wealth tax compared to unmarried male householders (31 percent) and unmarried female householders (37 percent). However, female-headed households would see their overall tax bill grow somewhat more in percentage terms than either of the other two household types.

As in the 1989 simulations, non-Hispanic white families would pay the highest wealth tax rate—0.8 percent. The "other" racial group (mainly Asian Americans) would face the second highest rate (0.6 percent), followed by Hispanics (0.2 percent) and non-Hispanic African Americans (0.1 percent). Whereas 47 percent of white families would pay some wealth tax, only 34 percent of "others," 16 percent of Hispanic families, and 17 percent of African-American families would be subject to this tax. Whites, Hispanics, and the "other" racial group would see about the same proportionate increase in their overall tax bill (5 percent), while African Americans would see their total federal taxes rise by only one percent.

As in the 1989 simulations, the distributional effect of the tax system is measured by the change in the Gini coefficient. Among all families, the Gini coefficient for pretax income is 0.531 in 1998, while the Gini coefficient for income after income taxes is 0.507. Adding the Swiss wealth tax to the personal income tax results in a further reduction of the Gini coefficient to only 0.505. The main reason, as in the 1989 simulations, is the small amount of revenue generated by the Swiss-style wealth tax.

9

Concluding Remarks

The pronounced rise in wealth inequality in the United States during the 1980s and 1990s creates some urgency in policy remedies. The most telling statistic is that virtually all the growth in (marketable) wealth between 1983 and 1998 accrued to the top 20 percent of households. Indeed, the bottom 40 percent of households saw its wealth decline in absolute terms. This was compounded by the stark reality of a growing proportion of households with zero or negative net worth. The results are very similar for financial wealth.

What, if anything, should be done about this? If one policy goal is to moderate the rising inequality of recent years, direct taxation of wealth is one proposed remedy.[1] This would compensate for the reduced progressivity of the income tax system. The 1980s witnessed falling marginal tax rates on income, particularly for the rich and very rich. Though the 1993 budget bill passed by Congress and signed into law by President Clinton raised the marginal income tax rates on the very rich, they are still considerably lower than at the beginning of the 1980s (and much lower than in the 1960s). President Bush is currently (as of February 2001) proposing to once again reduce the marginal tax rates on upper income families.

Currently, wealth is taxed in only two forms on the federal level: estate taxes (at death) and capital gains taxes (on realized capital gains). Eleven OECD countries currently have direct taxation on wealth (three others have had such a system in the past), and most of these are in conjunction with a death tax and a capital gains tax.

What do the simulation results of the previous chapter suggest? First, the current personal income tax system in the United States helps mitigate the disparities in earnings, but its overall effects are modest (indeed, they would probably appear even smaller if full information were available on itemized deductions and income adjustments). Second, of the three wealth tax systems considered, only the Swedish system has any noticeable equalizing effect, and even in this case the result is similarly modest. This is true even though the Swedish wealth tax would increase total tax revenues (over and above the personal income tax) by 74 percent. The German system would increase tax revenues by 15 percent, and the Swiss system would increase them by 8 percent in 1989 but only by 7 percent in 1998—in all cases, too small to have much distributional impact.

Third, these three wealth taxes have some desirable features from a demographic standpoint. All three tend to fall proportionately more on older families than on younger ones; more on married couples than on singles; and more on whites than on nonwhites (whites are much wealthier than nonwhites). Moreover, the equalizing effects of the wealth taxes are greater among older families, married couples, and whites.

Fourth, even the very modest Swiss-style system would have yielded an additional $38 billion of revenue in 1989 and $52 billion in 1998. In light of the demands on the federal budget, such a tax could be valuable indeed. In spite of the proposed tax's potency as a revenue-raising tool, only 3 percent of families would see their federal tax bill rise by more than 10 percent. In 1998, only 8 percent would have paid an additional $300 or more of taxes. In conclusion, a direct wealth taxation system such as Switzerland's could ease the country's budgetary strains and provide greater equity across generational, racial, and familial categories. These characteristics argue in favor of its adoption in the United States.

Other Rationales for Wealth Taxation. Besides its desirable effects with regard to equity and revenue, are there any other characteristics of wealth taxation that may argue in its favor? Two other arguments have been advanced in support of a wealth tax. First, beyond considerations of overall ("vertical") equity, some have argued that a wealth tax can be justified in terms of "taxable capacity." Income alone is not a sufficient gauge of well-being or of the ability to pay taxes. The possession of wealth, over and above the income it yields directly, must be figured into the calculation. Two families with identical incomes but different levels of wealth are not equivalent in terms of their well-being, since a wealthier family will have more independence, firmer security in times of economic stress (such as that occasioned by unemployment, illness, or family breakup), and readier access to consumer credit. Greater wealth thus confers on the affluent family a larger capacity to pay taxes; in the interests of "horizontal equity," wealth should be taxed directly, as well as income.

A second argument is that an annual wealth tax may induce individuals to transfer their assets from less productive uses to more productive ones. A tax on wealth may provide an incentive to switch from low-yielding investments to high-yielding ones in order to offset the additional taxes. For example, a wealth tax based on the market value of property might induce neglectful owners to seek to realize potential returns through development, renovation, or sale. Likewise, a wealth tax might induce individuals to seek more income-generating assets in place of conspicuous consumer durables such as luxury cars and yachts. A direct wealth tax has the added feature that it may inhibit the avoidance of income taxes by encouraging investors to switch assets into income-yielding forms.

It should be noted, too, that existing wealth taxation in the United States works poorly. The estate tax has historically been an extremely porous tax (some refer to it as a "voluntary" tax). The thresholds have been raised over time (from $50,000 in 1916, when the estate tax was first instituted, to $60,000 in 1942, then to $175,000 in 1981, to $600,000 in 1987, and to $675,000 today),[2] so that only a very small percentage of estates (typically on the order of 1 or 2 percent) have been subject to estate tax. The threshold is currently scheduled to rise to $1,000,000 by 2006. President Bush has proposed the complete elimination of the estate and gift tax over the next ten years.

Estate taxes on assets can even today be avoided altogether by setting up a trust fund with children or other desired "heirs" as beneficiaries (though provisions for such trusts were tightened up in the 1993 federal tax legislation). Moreover, gift exclusions allow a considerable amount of wealth to be passed on, before death, exempt from taxation. In addition, there are the usual problems of underreporting, valuation of assets (how to value a family business?), and compliance.

Finally, the estate tax system has a provision that capital gains on assets are essentially excluded from consideration. Normally, realized capital gains are counted as part of the taxable base in computing income taxes. However, if an asset is not sold and winds up in an estate, the capital gains are forgiven by the tax authorities. This loophole by itself probably more than equals the total revenue collected by the estate tax system. Given the history of estate taxes in this country and the vested interest of the wealthy in maintaining the current system (not to speak of the estate planners and lawyers who profit from the system), it may be easier politically to institute a new wealth tax than to try to revamp the existing estate tax regime.

COUNTERARGUMENTS

Perhaps the strongest argument against direct wealth taxation is that it will inhibit savings and lower capital investment. One unavoidable implication of wealth taxation is that the (after-tax) return to capital will be lowered. By exerting a strong disincentive on the already low U.S. savings rate, it may simply encourage increased consumption. Another possibility is that a wealth tax, by lowering the after-tax rate of return on financial assets, may encourage families to invest in nonfinancial assets, such as certain forms of real estate, collectibles, precious metals, luxury items, and the like. The search for greater opacity to thwart the Internal Revenue Service could perversely result in shifting of household portfolios to unproductive uses; though, as suggested earlier, one can reasonably argue the opposite case—that taxing both income-yielding and non–income-yielding forms of wealth will induce households to shift to higher-yielding assets.

One simple, though relatively crude, way of addressing this issue is to compare the average savings rates of countries with direct wealth taxes to those without such taxes. On the basis of OECD national accounts data, within both sets of countries there is large variation in average household savings rates over the period 1980–90.[3] Among those with a wealth tax, savings rates range from 4.0 percent for Spain to 8.2 percent for Germany, 9.1 percent for the Netherlands, and 10.5 percent for Switzerland. Among those without a wealth tax, figures range from 3.6 percent for the United Kingdom to 5.7 percent for the United States and 11.6 percent for Japan. The average savings rates among countries with a wealth tax is 8.0 percent, and that for countries without a wealth tax is 9.8 percent. It is far from clear that taxation of wealth explains these differences. Is the high savings rate in Japan due to low taxation of wealth? On the surface, at least, there appears to be no strong evidence that the presence of a wealth tax inhibits savings.

A second potential problem stemming from a wealth tax is capital flight. By inserting a wedge between what an asset earns and what the owner receives, a tax understates the return in the owner's eyes and encourages the owner to look for higher returns elsewhere. This argument applies to every tax, however, and if capital indeed moved like quicksilver, it would render any taxation of capital and wealth all but impossible. The very fact that the wealth tax proposal presented in the next section is based on the Swiss model suggests that capital flight is unlikely to be a serious concern. Like Switzerland, the United States is a safe haven for international wealth, a status unlikely to be threatened by the very low tax rates suggested here.

A WEALTH TAX FOR THE UNITED STATES

The time now is ripe for the introduction of a personal tax on wealth holdings. The statistics point to an enormous degree of inequality in household net worth in this country today, and an even greater degree in terms of household financial wealth. On the grounds of (horizontal) equity, a combination of annual income and the current stock of wealth provides a better gauge of the ability to pay taxes than income alone. Moreover, there is no evidence from other advanced economies that the imposition of a modest direct tax on household wealth has had a deleterious effect on personal savings or overall economic growth. In fact, there are arguments to the contrary, that such a tax may induce a more efficient allocation of household wealth toward more productive uses. Finally, the possibility that such a levy might promote capital flight is not borne out by the evidence.

Most appropriate for the United States would be a wealth tax modeled after the Swiss system. The basic exclusion could begin at $100,000. The marginal tax structure might look as follows: 0.05 percent applied to household wealth valued from $100,000 to $199,999; 0.10 percent from $200,000 to $349,999; 0.15 percent from $350,000 to $499,999; 0.20 percent from $500,000 to $749,999; 0.25 percent from $750,000 to $999,999; and 0.30 percent for $1,000,000 and above. As in the Swiss system, all household effects, pensions, and annuities would be excluded.[4] In addition, the rules would provide a $10,000 exemption on automobiles (that is, only expensive cars would be subject to the tax).

The wealth tax would be fully integrated with the personal income tax. The same tax form could be used for both. The family would be required to list the value of all assets and debts on a new subsidiary form (say, "Schedule W"). Verification of most of the assets and debts would be administratively easy to implement. Insofar as banks and other financial institutions provide records (Form 1099) to the Internal Revenue Service (IRS) that list interest payments, such documents could be modified to also include the value of the interest-bearing accounts as of a certain date (say, December 31). A similar procedure could be applied to dividend forms. Moreover, financial institutions that provide the Internal Revenue Service with information on mortgage payments made by households could now add the value of the outstanding mortgage. Other types of loans (and loan payments) could be similarly recorded by these institutions. Insurance companies could provide the IRS with statements on the value of life insurance equity (they already send these to individuals).

The two main stumbling blocks are establishing the current market value of owner-occupied housing (and other real estate) and the valuation of unincorporated businesses. For the former, there are several possible solutions, some of which are currently in use in other countries. The family could be asked to estimate the current market value (as is now done in household surveys). Alternatively, it could be asked to list the original purchase price and date of purchase, and the IRS could use a regional (or locale-specific) price index based on housing survey data to update the value. Another method would ask residents to provide the figure for assessed valuation of the property, and the IRS could provide a locale-specific adjustment factor, based on periodic survey data, to estimate current market value.

For unincorporated businesses, the simplest technique is to accumulate the value of individual assets invested in the business over time (these figures are already provided in Schedule C of the personal tax return). Another possibility is to capitalize the net profit figures (also provided on Schedule C), as the Swiss currently do.

Calculations show that such a tax structure would yield an average tax rate on household wealth (as of 1998) of 0.2 percent. Previous work indicates that the real rate of return on household wealth over the period from 1962 to 1998 averaged 3.2 percent per year.[5] Thus, the new tax regime would reduce the average yield on household assets by only 6 percent. Even the top marginal tax rate of 0.3 percent would reduce the average yield on personal wealth by only 9 percent. These figures suggest that disincentive effects, if any, on personal savings would be very modest.

Would such a tax be popular? Of course, no additional payment of taxes is likely to be cheered by the American people. But the proposed wealth tax would affect a very small percentage of the population. Only 3 percent of American families would see their overall personal tax bill (combining income and wealth taxes) rise by more than 10 percent. Only 8 percent would pay $300 or more of additional taxes. A full 78 percent would see their tax bill rise by no more than 1 percent, if at all. (In fact, two-thirds of households would fall below the $100,000 threshold and would therefore be exempted from paying.)

About $55 billion would be raised from levying such a tax in 2001 (somewhat less than would be raised by an exact copy of the Swiss system). This is not a large amount, representing about 3 percent of total federal tax receipts. However, on the margin, such additional revenue could be critical. Even at this writing, there are many programs that could benefit from an additional injection of tax revenue—such as expanded Temporary Assistance to Needy Families (TANF) coverage, Medicaid, food stamps, an expanded prescription drug plan in Medicare, increased unemployment insurance coverage, additional federal aid to education, and the like. A direct annual tax on personal wealth could thus be a valuable addition to the fiscal toolbox available to the federal government.

Appendix

Defining and Measuring Definitions of Wealth

This study uses three basic concepts of wealth: marketable wealth, "augmented wealth," and financial wealth.

Marketable wealth (or net worth)—HW (for household wealth)—is the current value of all marketable or fungible assets ("fungible" assets are defined as liquid assets plus stocks and other equities) less the current value of debts. Total assets are defined as the sum of: (1) the gross value of owner-occupied housing; (2) other real estate owned by the household; (3) cash and demand deposits; (4) time and savings deposits, certificates of deposit, and money market accounts; (5) government bonds, corporate bonds, foreign bonds, and other financial securities; (6) the cash surrender value of life insurance plans; (7) the cash surrender value of pension plans, including IRAs and Keogh plans; (8) corporate stock, including mutual funds; (9) net equity in unincorporated businesses; and (10) equity in trust funds. Total liabilities are the sum of: (1) mortgage debt, (2) consumer debt, and (3) other debt.

This first measure of wealth is used because the primary interest here is in wealth as a store of value and therefore a source of potential consumption. This is the concept that best reflects the level of well-being associated with a family's holdings. Thus, only assets that can be readily converted to cash are included.

A somewhat expanded variant of the first measure is HWX, which is defined as the sum of HW and consumer durables. Consumer durables include automobiles, televisions, furniture, household appliances, and the like. Although these items provide consumption services directly to the household, they are not easily marketed. In fact, the resale value of these items typically far understates the value of their consumption services to the household. However, this concept is useful for consistency with earlier studies, in particular, for the construction of a long-term time-series for the United States.[1]

A wider definition of household wealth will often add some valuation of pension rights, from both public and private sources, to marketable wealth. One of the major developments in the postwar period among industrialized countries has been the enormous growth in both public and private pension systems. Even though such pension funds are not in the direct control of individuals or families, they are a source of future income to families and thus may be perceived as a form of family wealth. Moreover, as Martin Feldstein has argued, insofar as families accumulate "traditional" wealth to provide for future consumption needs, the growth of such pension funds may have offset private savings and hence traditional wealth accumulation.[2] Such a measure may thus provide a better gauge of potential future consumption.

The second major concept used here is "augmented wealth," or AW, defined as the sum of household wealth (HW), pension wealth, and Social Security wealth.[3] Pension wealth is defined as the present value of discounted future pension benefits. In similar fashion, Social Security wealth is defined as the present value of the discounted stream of future Social Security benefits. A variant of AW is AWX, defined as the sum of HWX and retirement (pension and

Social Security) wealth. This concept is also employed for consistency with earlier studies.[4]

The third concept is financial wealth, FW, defined as net worth minus net equity in owner-occupied housing (the difference between the value of the property and its outstanding mortgage debt). Financial wealth is a more "liquid" concept than marketable wealth, since one's home is difficult to convert into cash in the short term. It thus reflects the resources that may be directly available for consumption or various forms of investments.

DATA AND MEASUREMENT

Data on the size distribution of household wealth in the United States are available principally from estate tax records and cross-sectional household surveys. The existing information can be pieced together to document the historical trends. A reasonably consistent series of estate tax records for the very wealthy collected nationally exists for selected years between 1922 and 1986. Comparative estimates of household wealth inequality are also provided from seven surveys conducted by the Federal Reserve Board, in 1962, 1983, 1986 (a special follow-up of the 1983 survey), 1989, 1992, 1995, and 1998. As indicated, these are based on stratified samples and are reasonably consistent over time.[5] In addition, a figure for 1979 is obtained from the Income Survey and Development Program (ISDP) of that year.

MARKETABLE WEALTH

There are three principal sets of studies that have constructed time-series from these data. The first, by Robert Lampman, covers the years from 1922 through 1953;[6] the second, by James D. Smith, provides concentration figures for the period from 1953 to 1976;[7] and the third, by Edward N. Wolff and Marcia Marley, constructs new estimates for the 1922–81 period.[8] The Lampman data and the Smith data are each internally consistent, using the same accounting conventions and the same set of national balance sheet estimates throughout. The Wolff-Marley study provides a consistent accounting framework and consistent set of national balance sheet totals in order to reconcile the Lampman and Smith estimates.

Table A-1 shows the original results of the Wolff-Marley series. These estimates are based on the Lampman data and the Smith results. The estate files used by Lampman and Smith do not include all assets, and the authors used different assumptions concerning pensions and trusts.[9] Another asset, life insurance, is overstated in the estate files (since it is reckoned at its face value rather than its cash surrender value), a problem that both Lampman and Smith appreciated and made adjustments for. Another difference is that Lampman's concentration estimates are based on estimates of aggregate household wealth prepared by Raymond W. Goldsmith,[10] while Smith's estimates used aggregate data from Richard and Nancy Ruggles.[11]

In order to derive a more consistent series on household wealth concentration, Wolff and Marley made a series of adjustments to the Lampman and Smith figures. First, they used consistent aggregate household balance sheet totals to derive the concentration estimates. Second, imputations were provided for the assets that were left out of the estate files, particularly trusts, and estimates of pensions and insurance values were standardized. Moreover, an additional data point was added to the series for 1981 on the basis of a study by Marvin Schwartz.[12]

The first column of Table A-1 shows the resulting series for the share of total assets held by the top 1 percent of asset owners and the second column shows the same for the share of net worth owned by the top 1 percent of wealth holders. The wealth concept used here is marketable wealth including consumer durables (HWX). Concentration figures are slightly higher based on net worth rather than on total assets, since relative indebtedness (the debt-equity ratio) is higher for poorer individuals than richer ones.[13]

The estate files represent the wealth of the deceased. The wealth estimates for the living population are derived using the estate multiplier method, which divides the population by age and sex and weights the deceased from each group as registered by the estate files by the reciprocal of the survival probability for that group. The survival probabilities used are higher than those for the population at large, due to the longer expected life span of the wealthy. This method represents a point estimate that can have a very large variance, particularly for the young, since there are very few of them in the sample.

Estate estimates have been criticized by A. B. Atkinson and A. F. Shorrocks as overestimating the decline in inequality.[14] The reason is that estate estimates are based on the individual rather than on the household unit, and over the century, marital customs and relations have changed. Married women now inherit more wealth and have higher wealth levels than they did in 1900 or 1930. This reduces the individual concentration even if household wealth inequality does not change. For example, between 1929 and 1953, Lampman reported that the percentage of married women among the top wealth holders increased from 9 to 18 percent.

Column 3 of Table A-1 shows the estimates of the share of total assets owned by the top 1 percent of households. As mentioned, estate files record wealth for the individual, while the more interesting unit for welfare analysis is the household. Moreover, the increased tendency to divide wealth equally between household members will reduce the individual concentration estimates without changing household wealth concentration. In order to change the estate data to a household base, certain assumptions are required about the division of wealth within households. The series shown in column 3 of Table A-1 is based upon the set of assumptions that yielded the smallest concentration estimates.[15] A comparison of columns 1 and 3 indicates that concentration figures are considerably lower on the basis of the household unit than the individual unit. This is to be expected since a married couple typically mixes a relatively affluent spouse with a less wealthy one.

Estimates from nine other sources of wealth data are shown in the next two columns. These are all based on the household as the unit of observation. Six sources—the 1962 Survey of Financial Characteristics of Consumers (SFCC), the 1983 Survey of Consumer Finances (SCF), the 1989 SCF, the 1992 SCF, the 1995 SCF, and the 1998 SCF—were conducted under the auspices of the Federal Reserve Board and include a high-income supplement. Imputations were made for missing values, and each sample has been aligned to the national balance sheet totals for that year to ensure greater consistency.[16]

The 1969 figure is derived from the MESP file, a synthetic database that is also fully aligned to the national balance sheet totals of that year.[17] The 1979 figure is based on the Daniel B. Radner and Denton R. Vaughan calculations from the 1979 ISDP,[18] which have then been benchmarked to the 1969 figure on the basis of a Pareto interpolation. Estimates are also available from the 1986 SCF, which resurveyed the families included in the 1983 SCF sample. Though there was a substantial "dropout rate" among the survey respondents, research by Robert B. Avery and Arthur B. Kennickell does provide some comparative estimates of wealth concentration in the two years.[19] The ten figures in column 5 of Table A-1 are all based on relatively comparable data sources.

To combine column 5 with the Wolff-Marley series, an overlapping year is necessary. Fortunately, two such "Rosetta stones" are provided, for 1962 and 1969. A comparison of columns 3 and 4 for 1962 reveals that the share of total assets owned by the top 1 percent of households is estimated to be considerably higher on the basis of the SFCC (29.9 percent) than on the basis of the estate tax series (22.1 percent). One possible reason for this difference is the conservative assumption used in converting the estate data to a household base. If it was instead assumed that all married men in the estate sample of top wealth holders had wedded women with wealth, the concentration estimates would have been higher, but not enough to account for the difference.[20] Another likely reason for the discrepancy between the estate and survey estimates is that there may be a serious underreporting problem in the estate data.[21]

Column 6 of Table A-1 shows the new series for the share of net worth owned by the top 1 percent of households from 1922 to 1998. Figures for the years 1962, 1969, 1979, 1983, 1986, 1989, 1992, 1995, and 1998 are based on the survey data sources. Other years, with the exception of 1933 and 1981, are calculated as column 3 multiplied by the ratio of the 1962 SFCC figure for the share of household net worth in column 5 (31.8 percent) and the estate tax figure for the share of household assets in column 3 (22.1 percent)—a ratio of 1.44. A similar procedure applied to the 1969 data yields almost the same ratio (1.43), which provides some confidence in this benchmarking procedure. Figures for 1933 and 1981 are interpolated on the basis of column 1.

The estimates of the "New Series" in column 6 show a high concentration of wealth throughout the period from 1922 to 1998. A quarter or more of total wealth was owned by the top 1 percent in each of these years except 1976 and 1981. A comparison of the two end points reveals similar concentration figures: 36.7 percent in 1922 and 34.9 percent in 1989. However, this comparison hides important trends over the period.

Between 1922 and 1929 there was a substantial increase in wealth concentration, from 37 to 44 percent (also see Figure 3-1). Wealth inequality in 1929 was at a high point (and probably at its peak for the twentieth century). The Great Depression saw a sizable drop in inequality, with the share of the top percentile falling to 33 percent, but by 1939 the concentration level was almost the same as it was in 1922. There followed a substantial drop in inequality between 1939 and 1945, a result of the leveling effects of World War II, and a more modest decline between 1945 and 1949.

The share of wealth held by the richest 1 percent of households showed a gradual upward trend from 27 percent in 1949 to a peak of 34 percent in 1965. There followed a rather pronounced fall in wealth inequality lasting until 1979. Between 1965 and 1972, the share of the top percentile fell from 34 to 29 percent, and then from 29 to 20 percent between 1972 and 1976.[22] The main reason for the decline in concentration over this four-year period is the sharp drop in the value of corporate stock held by the top wealth

TABLE A-1
PERCENT SHARE OF TOTAL MARKETABLE
HOUSEHOLD WEALTH HELD BY THE RICHEST 1 PERCENT
OF WEALTH HOLDERS IN THE UNITED STATES, 1922–1998[a]

WOLFF-MARLEY SERIES[b]

| | INDIVIDUALS | | HOUSEHOLDS |
YEAR	TOTAL ASSETS (1)	NET WORTH (2)	TOTAL ASSETS (3)
1922	34.0		25.5
1929	37.2		30.7
1933	31.3		
1939	38.1		25.3
1945	28.9		20.7
1949	25.7		18.8
1953	28.1	28.4	21.7
1958	27.0	27.7	20.0
1962	30.1	31.1	22.1
1965	31.9	33.6	23.9
1969	29.0	30.2	21.6
1972	28.6	29.8	20.2
1976	18.9	19.1	12.7
1979			
1981	23.6		
1983			
1986			
1989			
1992			
1995			
1998			

a. The concept used here is marketable wealth, including consumer durables (HWX).

b. Source: Wolff and Marley (1989), Tables 5, 6, 7, and 8. The results are based on the "W2" series, which is comparable to HWX. Figures on the share of assets owned by the top 1 percent of households (column 3) are lower bound estimates.

c. Sources: 1962 figures from the Survey of Financial Characteristics of Consumers (SFCC); 1979 figures from Radner and Vaughan (1987), based on the Income Survey and Development

OTHER SOURCES[c]		NEW SERIES HOUSEHOLDS	
HOUSEHOLDS		NET WORTH (HWX)	AUGMENTED WEALTH (AWX)[d]
TOTAL ASSETS (4)	NET WORTH (5)	(6)	(7)
		36.7	34.3
		44.2	41.1
		33.3	28.7
		36.4	30.2
		29.8	22.0
		27.1	20.7
		31.2	23.1
		28.8	20.4
29.9	31.8	31.8	21.9
		34.4	23.3
	30.8	31.1	20.9
		29.1	19.0
		19.9	13.3
	20.5	20.5	12.9
		24.8	15.5
	30.9	30.9	19.0
	31.9	31.9	19.3
	34.2	34.2	20.3
	34.0	34.0	19.8
	35.3	35.3	20.2
	34.9	34.9	19.6

Program (ISDP), where the share of wealth of the top 1 percent of households is estimated using a Pareto distribution; and 1983, 1986, 1989, 1992, 1995, and 1998 figures from the Survey of Consumer Finances (SCF).

d. Source: Wolff and Marley (1989), Table 6. The results are based on the "W4" series, where W4 is defined as marketable wealth W2 plus pension reserves and Social Security wealth.

holders. The total value of corporate stock owned by the richest 1 percent fell from $491 billion in 1972 to $297 billion in 1976.[23] Moreover, this decline appears to be attributable to the steep decline in share prices rather than a divestiture of stock holdings.

Wealth inequality appears to have bottomed out some time during the late 1970s. A sharp increase in wealth concentration occurred between 1979 and 1981, from a 21 percent share to a 25 percent share; again from 1981 to 1983, from a 25 percent share to a 31 percent share; and then once more between 1983 and 1989, from 31 to 34 percent. A further though more modest rise is evident in the 1990s, to 35 percent in 1998. This sharp rise in the concentration of household wealth paralleled the growth in income inequality evident during the 1980s and 1990s.[24]

RETIREMENT WEALTH

The last column of Table A-1 shows the "New Series" for the share of augmented household wealth, AWX (including consumer durables), owned by the top 1 percent of wealth holders. A similar procedure is used to develop this series as was done for HWX. The original source is the Wolff-Marley W4 series, where W4 is defined to include full pension reserves, which are reported in the aggregate data sources, as well as imputations for Social Security wealth.[25] However, one major difficulty is that there is very little information concerning the percentage of total pensions owned by the top wealth holders. In the Wolff-Marley paper, alternative assumptions were made about this share, ranging from a maximum of 15 percent to a minimum of 3 percent for the top 1 percent of wealth holders. The different assumptions had little effect on total wealth concentration. In the estimates reported for W4, it was assumed that the share of total pension wealth held by the top percentile of wealth holders declined over the course of the twentieth century because of the increase in pension coverage throughout the period.

Direct imputations of pension and Social Security wealth were made for the 1962 SFCC, the 1969 MESP, the 1983 SCF, and the

1989 SCF microdata files.[26] These estimates were used for the "New Series" for AWX shown in column 7.[27] Figures for W4 from 1922 through 1976 were then benchmarked against the 1962 estimate derived from the SFCC. Other years were filled in by interpolation.

The addition of pension and Social Security wealth has had a significant effect on measured wealth inequality (see also Figure 3-1). Because of the growth over time in pension and Social Security wealth, particularly the latter, in relation to marketable wealth, the gap between the HWX and the AWX series widens over time, from 2 percentage points in 1922 to 15 percentage points in 1998. However, the time patterns are almost identical. Wealth concentration based on the AWX series showed a sharp increase between 1922 and 1929; a substantial decline from 1929 to 1933; an increase between 1933 and 1939; a significant decrease between 1939 and 1945; a fairly flat trend from 1945 through 1972; a sharp decline from 1972 to 1976; and then a substantial rise between 1979 and 1989. In this case, inequality leveled off in the 1990s. The increase on the basis of augmented wealth during the 1980s, 6 percentage points, appears more muted than the comparable figure for marketable wealth, 15 percentage points.

METHODOLOGICAL NOTES ON THE MEASUREMENT OF WEALTH

In most industrialized countries today, there are now official estimates of the size distribution of household income. In the United States, for example, the Census Bureau conducts an annual survey in March, called the Current Population Survey, which provides detailed information on individual and household earnings and income. On the basis of these data, the U.S. Census Bureau constructs its estimates of both family and household income inequality. Moreover, the Current Population Survey has been conducted in the United States since 1947. As a result, there exists a consistent time-series on household income distribution for the United States that covers more than half a century.

Unfortunately, there do not exist comparable data on the size distribution of household wealth for the United States or, for that matter, for any other country in the world. There are no official household surveys conducted on an annual basis for this purpose. As a result, researchers in this field have had to make estimates of household wealth inequality from a variety of sources, which are often inconsistent. Compounding this problem is the fact that household wealth is much more heavily concentrated in the upper percentiles of the distribution than is income. Thus, unless surveys or data sources are especially designed to cover the top wealth groups in a country, it is easy to produce biased estimates of the size distribution of wealth. The end result is that estimates of household wealth distribution are less reliable than those for income distribution.

There are correspondingly many more methodological problems associated with household wealth data than with income data. These include problems concerning: asset coverage, the unit of observation, underreporting, sampling frame, and institutional differences in wealth ownership over time. Estimates of the size distribution of household wealth are quite sensitive to each of these considerations. As a result, it is precarious to compare inequality figures between different data sources. This is particularly true in making international comparisons. However, it is still possible to develop time trends on the basis of a single data source and to combine such time trends if benchmark estimates are available for the same years.

The principal data sources on household wealth will be described first in order to see how these considerations come into play. There have been five such sources: estate tax data, household survey data, wealth tax data, income capitalization techniques, and synthetic data sources. Each has its characteristic advantages and disadvantages.

Estate Tax Data

Estate tax data was the first major source of data used for wealth analysis. Estate tax records are actual tax returns filed for probate.

Such data have a great degree of reliability, since they are subject to scrutiny and audit by the state. Their main limitation, in the United States at least, is that the threshold for filing is relatively high, so that only a small proportion of estates (typically, 1 percent or so) are required to file returns.[28] Another difficulty with these data is that the sample consists of decedents. As a result, various assumptions must be used to construct "estate multipliers" in order to infer the distribution of wealth among the living. Insofar as mortality rates are inversely correlated with wealth (that is, the rich tend to live longer), the resulting multipliers can be biased. Moreover, the resulting estimated distribution of wealth is by individual rather than by family. Changing ownership patterns within families (for example, joint ownership of the family's house) can affect estimated wealth concentration. In addition, various other assumptions must be made to infer family wealth from estimates of individual wealth holdings.

Another problem involves underreporting and nonfiling for tax avoidance. Though the returns are subject to audit, the value of cash on hand, jewelry, housewares, and business assets is difficult to ascertain. Their value is typically understated in order to reduce the tax liability of the estate. Moreover, *inter vivos* transfers (that is, gifts between living individuals), particularly in anticipation of death, can bias estimates of household wealth among the living.[29]

HOUSEHOLD SURVEY DATA

The second principal source is the field survey. Its primary advantage is that it provides considerable discretion to the interviewer about the information requested of respondents. However, the major drawback is that information provided by the respondent is often inaccurate, and, in many cases, the information requested is not provided at all. Another problem is that because household wealth is extremely skewed, the very rich (the so-called upper tail of the distribution) are often considerably underrepresented in samples. During the 1980s and 1990s, the four major wealth surveys for the United States constructed on the basis of a representative sample have been the 1984, 1988, 1991, 1993, and 1995 Survey of Income and Program Participation (SIPP).[30]

An alternative is to use stratified samples, based typically on income tax returns, which oversample the rich. However, studies indicate that response error and nonresponse rates are considerably higher among the wealthy than among the middle class. Moreover, there are problems in "weighting" the sample in order to reflect the actual population distribution. There have, to date, been three major stratified samples for the United States, all conducted by the Federal Reserve Board.[31]

To give a sense of how much difference the choice of sampling frame makes in estimating wealth concentration, it is instructive to calculate the Gini coefficient (a standard measure of the concentration of wealth) from the 1983, 1989, and 1992 Survey of Consumer Finances (SCF) and from the 1984, 1988, 1991, and 1993 Survey of Income and Program Participation (SIPP) files. Both sets of calculations are based on nine wealth intervals as provided in the SIPP data and the same definition of net worth. The results are as follows:

GINI COEFFICIENT OF HOUSEHOLD WEALTH DISTRIBUTION

1983 SCF	0.80
1984 SIPP	0.69
1988 SIPP	0.69
1989 SCF	0.84
1991 SIPP	0.71
1993 SIPP	0.69
1992 SCF	0.77

The measured concentration is substantially higher on the basis of the stratified SCF files than on the basis of the representative SIPP files.[32] In general, the greater the coverage of the upper wealth groups in a sample, the higher is the degree of measured wealth concentration. As a result, one must remain rather suspicious of wealth inequality figures based on representative samples.[33]

WEALTH TAX DATA

A third source is wealth tax return data. A dozen or so European countries, including Germany, the Netherlands, and Sweden, assess taxes not only on current income but also on the stock of household wealth (see chapter 8 for more details). Though there is typically a threshold for paying wealth taxes, their coverage of the population can be considerably greater than that of estate tax returns. However, the measurement problems are similar to those of estate tax data. The filer has a great incentive to understate the value of the family's assets, or even not to report them. Moreover, the assets subject to tax do not cover the full range of household assets (for example, consumer durables are often excluded). In addition, the observational unit of measurement is the tax filing, which does not directly correspond to the family unit. Wealth tax data have been used extensively by Roland Spånt for an analysis of wealth trends in Sweden.[34]

INCOME CAPITALIZATION TECHNIQUES

The fourth type of wealth data is based on "income capitalization" techniques, which are usually applied to income tax return data. In this procedure, certain income flows, such as dividends, rents, and interest, are converted into corresponding asset values based on the average asset yield. For example, dividends are capitalized in order to estimate corporate stock holdings. This method also suffers from a number of defects. First, only assets with a corresponding income flow are covered in this procedure. Thus, owner-occupied housing, consumer durables, and idle land cannot be directly captured. Also, in the United States, state and local bonds cannot be estimated because their interest income is exempt from federal income taxes. Second, the estimation procedure rests heavily on the assumption that asset yields are uncorrelated with asset levels. Any actual correlation between the size of asset holdings and yields can produce biased estimates. Third, the observational unit is again based on the tax return. Various assumptions must be imposed in order to construct family wealth estimates from those of the tax filer. Charles Stewart conducted the earliest study on U.S. data using this technique.[35]

Synthetic Data Sources

Another source of wealth data involves combining two or more basic sources of data, as well as the merging and matching of data sets. There are two principal examples of this approach for the United States. Edward N. Wolff statistically matched 1969 U.S. tax return data from the Internal Revenue Service with the 1970 U.S. Census of Population survey data. Income capitalization was then applied to the tax return data to obtain the values of corresponding assets, and the census data were used to supply values for some of the missing assets, such as the value of owner-occupied housing.[36] Daphne T. Greenwood used a specially constructed data set in which individual income tax records were matched to family records in the 1973 Current Population Survey. Income capitalization was also applied to income flows to obtain corresponding asset values.[37] This approach has the advantage of combining the strengths of the basic data sources. However, the major pitfall is that the joint distributions of noncommon variables in the two data sources, inferred from statistical matches, are statistically unreliable.

Notes

CHAPTER 1: INTRODUCTION

1. U.S. Council of Economic Advisers (1994).

2. The source is U.S. Bureau of the Census, "Detailed Historical Income and Poverty Tables from the March Current Population Survey, 1947–1998," available on the Internet at http://www.census.gov/-hhes/income/histinc.

CHAPTER 2: WHY WEALTH?

1. Wealth is defined formally and in detail in the Appendix. To summarize very roughly and briefly, wealth is the difference between the value of assets and liabilities. Three variations of wealth are employed in this paper: Financial wealth includes assets (1)–(6) and (8)–(10) below; marketable wealth includes assets (1)–(10); augmented wealth includes all assets listed below. "Wealth" without an adjective refers to marketable wealth. Assets include (1) cash and demand deposits; (2) time and savings deposits, certificates of deposit, and money market accounts; (3) government bonds, corporate bonds, foreign bonds, and other financial securities; (4) the cash surrender value of life insurance plans; (5) the cash surrender value of pension plans, including IRAs and Keogh plans; (6) corporate stock,

including mutual funds; (7) the gross value of owner-occupied housing; (8) other real estate owned by the household; (9) net equity in unincorporated businesses; (10) equity in trust funds; (11) consumer durables; and (12) some valuation of pension rights, from both public and private sources. Total liabilities are the sum of (I) mortgage debt, (II) consumer debt, and (III) other debt.

2. Technically, there is a distinction between savings out of income, the difference between current income and current consumption, which is a national income and product account concept, and the revaluation of existing assets (capital gains and losses), which is a balance sheet concept.

3. In one attempt to explain the variation of wealth holdings by various factors, Greenwood (1987) found that income increased the amount of variation explained only from 6 to 17 percent. Wolff (1994) reported on the basis of 1989 wealth data that the inequality of wealth within income class was almost as pronounced as in the population as a whole.

4. Steuerle (1984).

5. Moreover, asset income is generally not well reported. Income statistics in the United States are generally based on census data (the Current Population Survey, primarily). Although coverage of wage and salary income is quite good, these data typically substantially understate property income such as dividends, interest, and rent. In some years, reported property income is less than half of what the national income and product accounts indicate it should be. It is therefore inadequate to use conventional income data to capture the distribution of asset income in this country.

6. See Radner and Vaughan (1987).

CHAPTER 3: HOUSEHOLD WEALTH INEQUALITY IN THE UNITED STATES

1. Household wealth has historically been and remains much more concentrated than household income, despite the rise in income inequality. In 1998, the top 1 percent of income recipients accounted for 17 percent of total household income, much less than the 38 percent of total wealth held by the top 1 percent of wealth holders. See, for example, the excellent review of income inequality trends by Levy and Murnane (1992).

2. Results in this section are based on the 1962 Survey of Financial Characteristics of Consumers (SFCC), the 1983 Survey of Consumer Finances (SCF), the 1989 SCF, the 1992 SCF, the 1995 SCF, and the 1998

SCF, all fully aligned with national balance sheet data. See Wolff (1994, 2001) for technical details. Data for earlier periods are reviewed in the Appendix. Results for 1989 have been revised from the first edition of the book because of the development of a new set of household weights by the Federal Reserve Board of Washington.

3. Distributions of wealth (and income) typically are organized into "quintiles"—that is, into groups of households arranged from poorest to wealthiest. The wealthiest 20 percent may be called the "top quintile." The bottom quintile is the least wealthy 20 percent of all households. The poorest 40 percent may be referred to as the "bottom two quintiles" or as the "bottom quintile and the next quintile."

4. If everyone were to receive a dollar increase in wealth, then the mean and median both would increase by a dollar as well. If the same total increase in wealth were enjoyed by the wealthiest person alone, average (mean) wealth still would rise by a dollar but the median would remain unchanged.

5. Median financial wealth also grew more slowly than mean financial wealth in the 1962–83 period, at about the same rate during the 1983–89 period, and faster than mean financial wealth in the 1989–98 period. Its growth increased from 0.6 percent per year in the 1962–83 period to 2.8 percent per year in both the 1983–89 and 1989–98 periods. Median household income grew slower than mean income in each of the three periods. Like median financial wealth, median income grew faster in 1983–89 (at 1.8 percent per year) than in 1962–83 (1.2 percent per year) but slower in the 1989–98 period (only 0.3 percent per year).

6. It should be noted that the concentration of income figures reported here on the basis of the 1983 and 1989 SCF are considerably higher than those based on the U.S. Census Current Population Surveys (CPS), noted in chapter 6. This is not surprising, for two reasons. First, the SCF has a high-income supplement and therefore provides better coverage of rich families than does the CPS (see the Appendix for an explanation of methodology). Second, the CPS "top-codes" income entries at $100,000 (the highest income interval is "$100,000 or more"), thus understating the income of the richest families, whereas the SCF has no top coding.

7. It should be noted that in these calculations, the households found in each group (say, the top quintile) may be different in the two years, due to economic mobility.

CHAPTER 4: THE CHANGING STRUCTURE OF
HOUSEHOLD WEALTH

1. Families are classified into age group on the basis of the age of the
family head.

2. See Modigliani and Brumberg (1954) for a discussion of the "life-
cycle model of savings."

3. It might seem odd that the relative wealth position of each of the
three age groups declined between 1989 and 1998. However, this statistical
artifact is due to the fact that share of total families in the above-average
age 70 and over group increased substantially over the period.

4. These numbers differ from the earlier edition of the book. In that
edition, families were classified into white and nonwhite, a group that
included Asians. In the new Table 4-1, families are classified as whites and
African Americans; Asians are excluded in this table. However, see the
footnotes to Table 4-1 regarding the treatment of Hispanic families.

5. Technically, IRAs can hold any type of asset, though in 1989 and
1998 they were predominantly in the form of bank deposits.

6. According to the Census, the home ownership rate increased from
55.0 percent in 1950 to 64.6 percent in 1975, but subsequently declined to
63.5 percent in 1985. The home ownership rate according to the SCF data
fell slightly from 63.4 percent in 1983 to 62.8 percent in 1989, but then
rebounded to 66.3 percent in 1998.

CHAPTER 5: COMPARISONS WITH OTHER COUNTRIES

1. Several problems with the estate data source and methodology for
the United Kingdom are discussed by Shorrocks (1987). First, the estate
multiplier method is likely to lead to some bias in estimated wealth shares
because of the positive correlation between wealth and life expectancy
(wealthier individuals tend to live longer). Second, the value of household
goods and small businesses are likely to be understated in estate data, since
their value is considerably greater when in use than when put up for sale.
Third, the value of life insurance policies is considerably greater in estates,
since they are fully paid out, than it is in comparable policies in the hands
of the living. Fourth, except for life insurance policies, the total value of
assets based on estate tax data falls far short of national balance sheet figures for the household sector.

2. The U.S. series is based on HWX for household unit. See the
Appendix and notes to Table A-1 for sources and methods for the United
States. Sources for the United Kingdom are: 1923–81—Atkinson,

Gordon, and Harrison (1989), Table 1; 1982–91—Board of Inland Revenue (1993), Series C, Table 13.5. Results are based on marketable wealth for adult individuals. The 1982–91 Inland Revenue Series is benchmarked to the 1923–1981 data. Sources for Sweden are: 1920–75—Spånt (1987), Tables 3.7, 3.8, and 3.11; 1975–92—Statistics Sweden (1994), Table 42. The unit is the household, and wealth is valued at market prices. The 1920–75 data are benchmarked to the Statistics Sweden series.

3. Because of the difficulties of comparing wealth data from different countries, a special study was undertaken to compare the distribution of household wealth in France and the United States. The main difficulty in the study was that survey data in the two countries cover different assets and liabilities (in fact, the French survey did not include any information on household debt). In order to compare the two distributions, it was necessary to create a "conformable" set of balance sheet accounts for the two countries.

The French data come from the 1986 Enquête sur les Actifs Financiers conducted by the Institut National de la Statistique et des Etudes Economiques (INSEE). The sample size is 5,602 families. This survey has a rather complex design, which is stratified by various sociodemographic characteristics. However, there is no special stratification by high income.

For the United States, the 1983 Survey of Consumer Finances (SCF), conducted by the Federal Reserve Board, is used. The 1983 SCF has a sample size of 4,262 families. Of these, 3,824 were randomly drawn and thus constitute a representative sample. The remaining 438 families constitute the so-called high-income supplement. These families were selected on the basis of their high income from a special sample created by the Internal Revenue Service from income tax returns. The U.S. survey data were then adjusted to conform to the coverage of the French survey data. Automobiles and other consumer durables were eliminated from the U.S. data, since these assets are not captured in the French data. Moreover, since household debt is not covered in the French survey, statistics are shown for total assets instead of net worth. See Kessler and Wolff (1991) for details.

4. There are two other possible explanations of the differences. The first is that there are differences in the degree of underreporting of assets in the two surveys. In other words, if holdings of particular assets by households are not accurately reported, this will distort the measured inequality from survey data. It proved feasible to check the potential bias for the U.S. survey data by aligning the U.S. survey data to national balance sheet totals. See Wolff (1987a) for details.

The second possible explanation is that the sampling frame differs between the two surveys. In particular, the U.S. data have a special component of high-income households that does not exist in the French data. It is well known that the better the coverage of high-income households, the higher is measured wealth inequality from such a survey. Thus, part of the reason for the finding of greater wealth inequality in the United States than in France may be the greater coverage of wealthy families in the U.S. data.

5. The source is Burkhauser, Frick, and Schwarze (1997). The estimates are derived from the German Socio-Economic Panel (GSOEP) and the U.S. Panel Survey of Income Dynamics (PSID/GSOEP) Equivalent Data File. The wealth figures exclude consumer durables.

6. Calculations for the United States are based on the 1983 Survey of Consumer Finances. The figures include the value of vehicles but exclude other consumer durables. The source for the Canadian data is Davies (1993), p. 162. The figures include the value of vehicles but exclude other consumer durables.

7. The source for the Japanese data is Bauer and Mason (1992), pp. 416–17. The 1981 figure is originally from Tachibanaki (1990) and is derived from the 1981 Family Saving Survey (FSS) and the 1981 Survey on Saving Behavior and Motivation (SSBM). The 1984 figures are originally from Takayama (1994) and are based on the 1984 National Survey of Family Income and Expenditure (NFIE). The value of major consumer durables is included in these estimates. The source for the Swedish data is Bager-Sjogren and Klevmarken (1993), pp. 208–10. The HUS figures are based on the survey, "Household Market and Non-market Activities" (HUS). The Statistics Sweden figures are originally from Jansson and Johansson (1988) and are based on a household survey conducted by Statistics Sweden.

8. See O'Higgins, Schmaus, and Stephenson (1989), Table 2, or Atkinson, Rainwater, and Smeeding (1995), for example.

9. See, for example, Smeeding and Rainwater (2001).

CHAPTER 6: WEALTH INEQUALITY VERSUS INCOME INEQUALITY

1. The basic data source is the Current Population Report series on shares of income held by families that runs from 1947 to 1998. The data are available on the Internet at the address: http://www.census.gov/hhes/income/histinc. The earlier data, from 1922 to 1949, are from Kuznets's (1953) series on the percentage share of total income received by the top percentiles of tax units. This series is benchmarked against the census figure for 1949.

2. My source for the data in this paragraph is Figure 3-4 above.

3. The source for the income data in this section is U.S. Bureau of the Census, "Detailed Historical Income and Poverty Tables from the March Current Population Survey, 1947–1998," available on the Internet at http://www.census.gov/hhes/income/histinc. Results are based on the household unit, including families and unrelated individuals. Statistics on family income alone, available from the same source, show almost identical trends.

4. Incomes of poor households have not fallen only because these households have worked more hours as more women have joined the workforce. Women's wages have been rising, but men with a high school education or less saw their real wages drop through the 1980s and 1990s.

5. This argument would not apply as readily to augmented household wealth (AW), since pension reserves are held mainly in the form of corporate stock shares and pension wealth is more widespread in the population than individual ownership of corporate stock. Moreover, even in the case of marketable wealth, which includes the surrender value of many types of defined contribution plans (steadily displacing defined benefit plans in private pensions over the last decade or so), the marketable wealth of middle-class families will be increasingly subject to fluctuations in the stock market.

6. A straightforward regression of a wealth inequality index, measured by the share of marketable wealth held by the top 1 percent of households (WLTH) on income inequality, measured by the share of income received by the top 5 percent of families (INC), and the ratio of stock prices (the Standard and Poor index) to housing prices (RATIO), with twenty-one data readings between 1922 and 1998, yields:

$$\text{WLTH} = 5.10 + 1.27 \text{ INC} + 0.26 \text{ RATIO}, R^2 = 0.64, N = 21$$
$$(0.9) \quad (4.2) \qquad (2.5)$$

with t-ratios shown in parentheses. Both variables are statistically significant (INC at the 1 percent level and RATIO at the 5 percent level) and with the expected (positive) sign. Also, the fit is quite good, even for this simple model.

The dominant factor in explaining changes in wealth concentration is income inequality. However, the movement in the ratio of stock to housing prices explains most of the increase in wealth inequality between 1949 and 1965 and the subsequent decline between 1965 and 1979 (particularly between 1972 and 1976). What about the 1980s and 1990s? From the regression results, almost two fifths (39 percent) of the increase in wealth concentration between 1981 and 1998 is attributable to the increase in income inequality and 29 percent to the increase of stock prices relative to housing prices. The remaining 29 percent is left unexplained.

CHAPTER 7: CURRENT SYSTEMS OF WEALTH TAXATION

1. A related tax is the property tax, levied on the value of all real property (buildings and land). Though this is often overlooked in current debates on tax reforms, the property tax is the third-largest source of household tax revenue and has been rising steeply in recent years. This tax is generally levied by local governments in this country and, as a result, will not be discussed in the present report. Of the twenty-four Organization of Economic Cooperation and Development (OECD) countries, all but Italy and Portugal have a separate tax on real property.

2. Gifts within three years of death are treated as transfers at death.

3. There are some complications that arise from capital losses and the carryover of capital losses from previous years, particularly in regard to short-term capital gains.

4. Most of the information in this section is garnered from the Organization of Economic Cooperation and Development (1988). The figures in this section are as of 1988 in most cases and are, of course, subject to change over time. The OECD has, unfortunately, not updated its survey. However, information garnered from statistical offices from a number of countries (Denmark, Germany, Norway, Sweden, and Switzerland, in particular) does not suggest any major change in the structure of their wealth tax.

5. Japan also had a direct wealth tax for a short period after World War II.

6. In Switzerland, the wealth tax is actually a provincial (canton) tax, so that provisions vary among cantons.

7. There is a technical issue related to debts on excluded assets. Since the wealth tax is based on the total value of assets less debts, the appropriate treatment would be to exclude debts on assets that are themselves excluded from the tax base. However, because of the difficulty of assigning specific debts (such as bank overdrafts) to specific assets, countries vary in their treatment of this problem.

8. Actually, in the U.S. estate tax system, preferential treatment is given to a spousal transfer in the form of a complete exemption. There is also a special, additional tax levied on generation-skipping bequests.

9. The source is U.S. Council of Economic Advisers (2001), p. 422. The estimated total federal receipts from the estate and gift tax in the year 2000 is $27.0 billion, or 1.4 percent of total (estimated) tax revenue.

Chapter 8: Simulations of Direct Wealth
Taxation in the United States

1. It should be noted that in the simulations all assets are appraised at market value (since this is the only valuation available).

2. The procedure was as follows: First, adjusted gross income (AGI) was estimated as the sum of all income items (excluding Social Security income). Second, the number of exemptions was computed. Third, the standard deduction was calculated. This is based on the filing status of the household and the number of persons aged 65 or older in the household. Fourth, taxable income was calculated by taking AGI minus the number of exemptions multiplied by $2,000 and subtracting the standard deduction. Federal income tax was then computed on the basis of the appropriate tax tables. After the initial run, the estimation procedure could be calibrated. Total individual federal income taxes collected in 1989 amounted to $445.7 billion (the source is the Council of Economic Advisors [1991], Table B77). The tax estimation used here produces a total tax figure for all households of $526.4 billion (an 18 percent discrepancy). The tax estimates were subsequently reduced by 18 percent to align with the actual figure. With this system, taxes were then recomputed in the same way, except in treating household wealth as an additional taxable item in accordance with the details of each of the three plans shown in Table 8-1.

3. Data problems include the following: (1) itemized deductions, particularly interest payments and state and local tax payments, cannot be included in the analysis; (2) the data analysis cannot incorporate capital gains in family income; (3) tax-exempt interest income is not excluded from AGI; and (4) any adjustments to income are not included in the computation of AGI. It is assumed that the net effect of these omitted adjustments is approximately captured by the 18 percent adjustment to tax revenues.

4. The revenue effect estimated on the basis of the Swiss system (2.2 percent of total U.S. tax revenues) is not very far out of line with the actual experience of that country; in 1985, the Swiss wealth tax accounted for 2.3 percent of total tax revenues in Switzerland. On the other hand, the relative revenue effects estimated from the German and particularly the Swedish system are much greater than the actual wealth tax yields in those countries. There are four possible reasons for the discrepancy in results. First, total tax revenues are a higher proportion of GNP in Germany (37 percent in 1988) and in Sweden (55 percent) than in the United States (30 percent). Second, household wealth holdings relative to income may be lower in Germany and Sweden than in the United States. Third, there may

be substantial tax evasion and avoidance in the two European countries. Fourth, in the case of Sweden at least, there is a cap on the joint income and wealth tax, which limits liability for the wealth tax for a large proportion of wealthy Swedish families because of the very high marginal tax rates on income that existed in the 1980s.

5. However, as indicated in the previous note, the incorporation of itemized deductions, tax preference items, and other income adjustments would make the effective tax rates on income considerably less progressive.

6. The source is: U.S. Council of Economic Advisers (2001), Table B-81. Accordingly, I reduced the tax estimates by 7 percent to align with the actual figure. However, as in the tax simulation for 1989, I still use the standard deduction in the tax calculations. As a consequence, the results still likely overstate the redistributional effects of the personal income tax system.

CHAPTER 9: CONCLUDING REMARKS

1. See David (1973) for one such proposal for the United States and Tait (1967) for the United Kingdom.

2. The ceiling was actually raised to $100,000 in 1926 but then lowered back to $50,000 in 1932.

3. Organization for Economic Cooperation and Development (1992). Technically, the savings rates are for the sector grouping households, non-profit institutions, and unincorporated businesses. The sample of countries includes all those listed in Table 7-1 except Denmark, Iceland, Ireland, Luxembourg, and Turkey.

4. Other, more subtle exclusions may be warranted as well. For example, provisions to protect old people living with low income in valuable family homes appear worthwhile. The law could, for example, postpone taxes on this wealth, incorporating them into estate taxes.

5. The source is Wolff (1999), with updated estimates.

APPENDIX

1. The inclusion of consumer durables can make a significant difference in estimated wealth concentration. For example, on the basis of the 1983 Survey of Consumer Finances, one can calculate a Gini coefficient of 0.80 and a share of wealth held by the top percentile of 34 percent for HW, and values of 0.74 and 31 percent, respectively, for HWX.

2. Feldstein (1974).

3. Technically, pension cash surrender value, which is already included in the calculation of HW, is then subtracted from this total to avoid double-counting.

4. Technical details on the estimation of retirement wealth can be found in Feldstein (1974, 1976) and Wolff (1987b, 1988, and 1992).

5. Another set of comparable estimates is also available from the U.S. Census Bureau's 1984, 1988, 1991, 1993, and 1995 Survey of Income and Program Participation (SIPP) data set. However, as suggested later, because the SIPP is a representative sample (and as such tends toward bias in measuring the uppermost echelons of the distribution, as opposed to a stratified sample designed to capture this segment more accurately), the wealth inequality estimates do not appear very reliable. See Wolff (1994) for further details.

6. Lampman (1962).

7. Smith (1984, 1987).

8. Wolff and Marley (1989).

9. For example, in Smith's estimates pensions are included only at their cash surrender value, and a large percentage of trusts—those that were not directly under the control of the deceased—are measured at their actuarial value since that is how they are measured in the estate files. On the other hand, Lampman used a wealth formula that includes the full value of pensions as well as trusts. Because of the fraction of trusts not included, Smith's reported concentration estimates are biased downward in relation to Lampman's.

10. Goldsmith (1962).

11. Ruggles and Ruggles (1982).

12. Schwartz (1983).

13. See Wolff (1994) for details.

14. Atkinson (1975); Shorrocks (1987).

15. See Wolff and Marley (1989) for details.

16. See Wolff (1987a) and Wolff (1994) for details.

17. See Wolff (1980) and Wolff (1983) for details.

18. Radner and Vaughan (1987).

19. Avery and Kennickell (1993).

20. See Wolff and Marley (1989), Appendix II, for details.

21. Perhaps somewhat coincidentally, the share of total assets and net worth owned by the top 1 percent of households in 1962, computed on the basis of the SFCC, lines up almost exactly with the share of total assets and net worth owned by the top 1 percent of individuals on the basis of the estate tax data. The same relation holds for 1969.

22. According to the original figures of Smith (1987), the share of net worth owned by the top 1 percent of wealth holders fell from 27.7 percent in 1972 to 19.2 percent in 1976. Schwartz (1984–85) reported a slightly higher share of net worth owned by the top percentile in 1976, 20.8 percent; Table A-1 uses Schwartz's figure rather than Smith's for the "New Series" in column 6.

23. See Smith (1987).

24. This trend is confirmed in the estate tax figures. According to Schwartz (1984–85), the share of total personal wealth held by the top 2.8 percent of the nation's adult population was 28 percent in 1982, and, according to Schwartz and Johnson (1990), the share held by the top 1.6 percent of the adult population was 28.5 percent in 1986.

25. See Wolff and Marley (1989) for details.

26. See Wolff (1987b) and Wolff and Marley (1989) for details.

27. The estimates shown here are based on the assumption that real average Social Security benefits grow by 2 percent per year over time.

28. In the United Kingdom, the threshold is considerably lower, so that the vast majority of estates file tax returns.

29. Estate tax data have been used by Atkinson and Harrison (1978), Shorrocks (1987), and Atkinson, Gordon, and Harrison (1989) for the United Kingdom; and Lampman (1962), Smith (1974, 1984, 1987), Smith and Franklin (1974), Wolff and Marley (1989), Scwharz (1984–85), and Schwarz and Johnson (1990) for the United States. The long-term time-series concentration estimates for Britain and the United States are based on estate tax data and the individual unit of account.

30. See U.S. Bureau of the Census (1986 and 1990a) for details on the 1984 and 1988 surveys, respectively. Information on the SIPP wealth supplements for 1991, 1993, and 1995 can be obtained from the U.S. Bureau of the Census' Web site: http://www.sipp.census.gov/sipp. See Anderson (1999) for details.

31. These are: the 1962 Survey of Financial Characteristics of Consumers—see Projector and Weiss (1966) for a description; the 1983 Survey of Consumer Finances—see Avery et al. (1984) for a description; the 1989 Survey of Consumer Finances—see Kennickell and Shack-Marquez (1992) for a description; the 1992 Survey of Consumer Finances—see Kennickell, McManus, and Woodburn (1996) for a description; the 1995 Survey of Consumer Finances—see Kennickell and Woodburn (1999) for a description; and the 1998 Survey of Consumer Finances.

32. It is unlikely that the differences in results can be accounted for by the difference in years, since the discrepancies are large between the 1983 SCF and the 1984 SIPP, as well as between the 1988 SIPP and the 1989 SCF, and both the 1991 and 1993 SIPP and the 1992 SCF.

33. See Wolff (1994) for more details.

34. Spånt (1987).

35. Stewart (1939).

36. Wolff (1980, 1982, and 1983).

37. Greenwood (1983, 1987).

Bibliography

Anderson, Joseph M. "The Wealth of U.S. Families: Analysis of Recent Census Data," U.S. Bureau of the Census, Survey of Income and Program Participation, Working Paper No. 233 (November 10, 1999).

Atkinson, A. B. "The Distribution of Wealth in Britain in the 1960s: The Estate Duty Method Reexamined." In James D. Smith, ed., *The Personal Distribution of Income and Wealth, Studies in Income and Wealth*, vol. 39 (New York: National Bureau of Economic Research, 1975).

Atkinson, Anthony B., James P. F. Gordon, and Alan Harrison. "Trends in the Shares of Top Wealth-Holders in Britain, 1923–81," *Oxford Bulletin of Economics and Statistics* 51, no. 3, August 1989: 315–32.

Atkinson, A. B., and A. J. Harrison. *Distribution of Personal Wealth in Britain* (Cambridge: Cambridge University Press, 1978).

Atkinson, Anthony B., Lee Rainwater, and Timothy Smeeding. *Income Distribution in Advanced Economies: The Evidence from the Luxembourg Income Study (LIS)* (Paris: OECD, 1995).

Avery, Robert B., and Arthur B. Kennickell. "U.S. Household Wealth:

Changes from 1983 to 1986." In Edward N. Wolff, ed., *Research in Economic Inequality,* vol. 4 (Greenwich, Conn.: JAI Press, 1993).

Avery, Robert B., Gregory E. Elliehausen, Glenn B. Canner, and Thomas A. Gustafson. "Survey of Consumer Finances, 1983." Board of Governors of the Federal Reserve System, Federal Reserve Bulletin 70, no. 3 (September 1984): 679–92.

Bager-Sjogren, Lars, and N. Anders Klevmarken. "The Distribution of Wealth in Sweden, 1984–1986." In Edward N. Wolff, ed., *Research in Economic Inequality,* vol. 4, "Studies in the Distribution of Household Wealth" (Greenwich, Conn: JAI Press, 1993): 203–24.

Bauer, John, and Andrew Mason. "The Distribution of Income and Wealth in Japan." *Review of Income and Wealth* 38, no. 4 (December 1992): 403–28.

Board of Governors of the Federal Reserve System. Survey of Financial Characteristics of Consumers. Washington, D.C., 1962. Database.

Board of Governors of the Federal Reserve System. Survey of Consumer Finances. Washington, D.C., 1983, 1986, and 1989. Databases.

Board of Inland Revenue (United Kingdom). Inland Revenue Statistics, 1993. (London: Her Majesty's Statistical Office, 1993).

Burkhauser, Richard V., Joachim R. Frick, and Johannes Schwarze. "A Comparison of Alternative Measures of Economic Well-Being for Germany and the United States." *Review of Income and Wealth* 43, no. 2 (June 1997): 153–72.

David, Martin. "Increased Taxation with Increased Acceptability: A Discussion of Net Worth Taxation as a Federal Revenue Alternative." *Journal of Finance* 28, no. 2 (May 1973): 481–95.

Davies, James B. "The Distribution of Wealth in Canada." In Edward N. Wolff, ed., *Research in Economic Inequality,* vol. 4, "Studies in the Distribution of Household Wealth" (Greenwich, Conn: JAI Press, 1993): 159–80.

Feldstein, Martin. "Social Security, Induced Retirement, and Aggregate Capital Accumulation." *Journal of Political Economy* 82, no. 5 (September/October 1974): 905–26. "Social Security and the

Distribution of Wealth." *Journal of the American Statistical Association* 71, no. 356 (December 1976): 800–07.

Goldsmith, Raymond W. *The National Wealth of the United States in the Postwar Period.* National Bureau of Economic Research. (Princeton, N.J.: Princeton University Press, 1962).

Greenwood, Daphne T. "An Estimation of U.S. Family Wealth and Its Distribution from Microdata, 1973." *Review of Income and Wealth,* series 29, no. 1 (March 1983): 23–43. "Age, Income, and Household Size: Their Relation to Wealth Distribution in the United States." In E. Wolff, ed., *International Comparisons of the Distribution of Household Wealth* (New York: Oxford University Press, 1987): 121–40.

Greenwood, Daphne T., and Edward N. Wolff. "Changes in Wealth in the United States, 1962–1983: Savings, Capital Gains, Inheritance, and Lifetime Transfers." *Journal of Population Economics* 5, no. 4 (1992): 261–88.

Jansson, K., and S. Johansson. *Formogenhetsfordelningen, 1975–1987* (Stockholm: Statistka Centralbyran, 1988).

Kennickell, Arthur B., Douglas A. McManus, and R. Louise Woodburn. "Weighting Design for the 1992 Survey of Consumer Finances." Federal Reserve Board of Washington (March 1996), Unpublished paper.

Kennickell, Arthur B., and J. Shack-Marquez. "Changes in Family Finances from 1983 to 1989: Evidence from the Survey of Consumer Finances." Board of Governors of the Federal Reserve System, *Federal Reserve Bulletin* 78, no. 1 (January 1992): 1–18.

Kennickell, Arthur B., and R. Louise Woodburn. "Consistent Weight Design for the 1989, 1992, and 1995 SCFs, and the Distribution of Wealth." *Review of Income and Wealth* 45, no. 2 (June 1999): 193–216.

Kessler, Denis, and Edward N. Wolff. "A Comparative Analysis of Household Wealth Patterns in France and the United States." *Review of Income and Wealth,* series 37, no. 3 (September 1991): 249–66.

Kuznets, Simon. *Shares of Upper Income Groups in Income and Savings* (New York: National Bureau of Economic Research, 1953).

Lampman, Robert. *The Share of Top Wealth-Holders in National Wealth, 1922–56.* (Princeton, N.J.: Princeton University Press, 1962).

Levy, Frank, and Richard Murnane. "Earnings Levels and Earnings Inequality." *Journal of Economic Literature* 30, no. 3 (September 1992): 133–81.

Modigliani, Franco, and Richard Brumberg. "Utility Analysis and the Consumption Function: An Interpretation of Cross-Section Data." In K. Kurihara, ed., *Post-Keynesian Economics* (New Brunswick, N.J.: Rutgers University Press, 1954).

O'Higgins, Michael, Guenther Schmaus, and Geoffrey Stephenson. "Income Distribution and Redistribution: A Microdata Analysis for Seven Countries." *Review of Income and Wealth,* series 35, no. 2 (June 1989): 107–32.

Organization for Economic Cooperation and Development. Taxation of Net Wealth, Capital Transfers and Capital Gains of Individuals (Paris: OECD, 1988).

Organization for Economic Cooperation and Development. National Accounts, Detailed Tables, 1978–1990, vol. 2 (Paris: OECD, 1992).

Pechman, Joseph A. *Who Paid the Taxes, 1966–1985?* (Washington, D.C.: The Brookings Institution, 1985).

Projector, Dorothy, and Gertrude Weiss. Survey of Financial Charactersitics of Consumers. Federal Reserve Technical Papers, Board of Governors of the Federal Reserve System, 1966.

Radner, Daniel B., and Denton R. Vaughan. "Wealth, Income, and the Economic Status of Aged Households." In Edward N. Wolff, ed., *International Comparisons of the Distribution of Household Wealth* (New York: Oxford University Press, 1987): 93–120.

Ruggles, Richard, and Nancy Ruggles. "Integrated Economic Accounts for the United States, 1947–1980." *Survey of Current Business* 62, no. 5 (May 1982): 153.

Schwartz, Marvin. "Trends in Personal Wealth 1976–1981." Internal Revenue Service, *Statistics of Income Bulletin* 3, no. 1 (Summer 1983): 1–26. "Preliminary Estimates of Personal Wealth, 1982: Composition of Assets." Internal Revenue Service, *Statistics of Income Bulletin* 4, no. 3 (Winter 1984–85): 1–17.

Schwartz, Marvin, and Barry Johnson. "Estimates of Personal Wealth,

1986." Internal Revenue Service, *Statistics of Income Bulletin* 9, no. 4 (Spring 1990): 63–78.

Shorrocks, A. F. "U.K. Wealth Distribution: Current Evidence and Future Prospects." In Edward N. Wolff, ed., *International Comparisons of the Distribution of Household Wealth* (New York: Oxford University Press, 1987): 29–50.

Smeeding, Timothy M., and Lee Rainwater. "Comparing Living Standards Across Nations: Real Incomes at the Top, the Bottom and the Middle." Jerome Levy Institute of Economics, Bard College, May 2001.

Smith, James D. "The Concentration of Personal Wealth in America, 1969." *Review of Income and Wealth,* series 20, no. 2 (June 1974): 143–80.

————"Trends in the Concentration of Personal Wealth in the United States, 1958–1976." *Review of Income and Wealth,* series 30, no. 4 (December 1984): 419–28.

————"Recent Trends in the Distribution of Wealth in the U.S.: Data, Research Problems, and Prospects." In Edward N. Wolff, ed., *International Comparisons of the Distribution of Household Wealth* (New York: Oxford University Press, 1987): 72–89.

Smith, James D., and Stephen Franklin. "The Concentration of Personal Wealth, 1922–1969." *American Economic Review* 64, no. 2 (May 1974): 162–67.

Spånt, Roland. "Wealth Distribution in Sweden: 1920–1983." In Edard N. Wolff, ed., *International Comparisons of the Distribution of Household Wealth* (New York: Oxford University Press, 1987): 51–71.

Statistics Sweden. *Income Distribution Survey in 1992.* (Örebo, Sweden: SCB Publishing Unit, 1994).

Steuerle, C. Eugene. "Realized Income and Wealth for Owners of Closely Held Farms and Businesses: A Comparison." *Public Finance Quarterly* 12 (October 1984): 407–24.

Stewart, Charles. "Income Capitalization as a Method of Estimating the Distribution of Wealth by Size Group." In *Studies in Income and Wealth,* vol. 3 (New York: National Bureau of Economic Research, 1939).

Tachibanaki, H. *Land Taxation Reform in Japan.* JEI Report no. 28A, Japan Economic Institute, Washington, D.C. (July 20, 1990).

Takayama, Noriyuki, "Household Asset- and Wealthholdings in Japan." In Yukio Noguchi and David A. Sie, eds., *Aging in the United States and Japan: Economic Trends* (Chicago: University of Chicago Press for the National Bureau of Economic Research, 1994): 85–108.

Tait, Alan A. *The Taxation of Personal Wealth* (Urbana, Ill.: University of Illinois Press, 1967).

U.S. Bureau of the Census. *Current Population Reports,* series P70, no. 7, "Household Wealth and Asset Ownership, 1984" (Washington, D.C.: U.S. Government Printing Office, 1986).

U.S. Bureau of the Census. *Current Population Reports,* series P70, no. 22, "Household Wealth and Asset Ownership, 1988" (Washington, D.C.: U.S. Government Printing Office, 1990[a]).

U.S. Bureau of the Census. *Current Population Reports,* series P60, no. 167, "Trends in Income by Selected Characteristics: 1947–1988" (Washington, D.C.: U.S. Government Printing Office, 1990[b]).

U.S. Bureau of the Census. *Current Population Reports,* series P60, no. 168, "Money Income and Poverty Status in the United States, 1989" (Washington, D.C.: U.S. Government Printing Office, 1990[c]).

U.S. Bureau of the Census. *Statistical Abstract of the United States, 1991,* 112th ed. (Washington, D.C.: U.S. Government Printing Office, 1991).

U.S. Bureau of the Census. *Survey of Income and Program Participation.* Washington, D.C., 1984, 1989. Databases.

U.S. Council of Economic Advisers. *Economic Report of the President.* (Washington, D.C.: U.S. Government Printing Office, various years).

Wolff, Edward N. "Estimates of the 1969 Size Distribution of Household Wealth in the U.S. from a Synthetic Database." In James D. Smith, ed., *Modeling the Distribution and Intergenerational Transmission of Wealth* (Chicago: University of Chicago Press, 1980).

————. "Effect of Alternative Imputation Techniques on Estimates of Household Wealth in the U.S. in 1969." In D. Kessler, A. Masson, and D. Strauss-Kahn, eds., *Accumulation et Repartition des Patrimoines.* (Paris: Economica, 1982).

———. "The Size Distribution of Household Disposable Wealth in the United States." *Review of Income and Wealth,* series 29 (June 1983): 125–46.

———. "Estimates of Household Wealth Inequality in the U.S., 1962–1983." Review of Income and Wealth, series 33, (September 1987[a]): 231–56.

———. "The Effects of Pensions and Social Security on the Distribution of Wealth in the United States." In Edward N. Wolff, ed., *International Comparisons of the Distribution of Household Wealth* (New York: Oxford University Press, 1987[b]): 208–47.

———. "Social Security, Pensions, and the Life Cycle Accumulation of Wealth: Some Empirical Tests." *Annales d'Economie et de Statistique,* no. 9 (January/March 1988): 199–226.

———. "Methodological Issues in the Estimation of Retirement Wealth." In D. Slottje, ed., *Research in Economic Inequality,* vol. 2 (Greenwich, Conn.: JAI Press, 1992): 31–56.

———. "Trends in Household Wealth in the United States during the 1980s." *Review of Income and Wealth,* series 40, no. 2 (June 1994): 143–74.

———. "International Comparisons of Wealth Inequality." *Review of Income and Wealth,* series 42, no. 4, December 1996: 433–51.

———. "Wealth Accumulation by Age Cohort in the U.S., 1962–1992: The Role of Savings, Capital Gains and Intergenerational Transfers." Geneva Papers on Risk and Insurance 24, no. 1, (January 1999): 27–49.

———. "Recent Trends in Wealth Ownership, 1983–1998." In Thomas M. Shapiro and Edward N. Wolff, eds., *Assets and the Disadvantaged: The Benefits of Spreading Asset Ownership* (New York: Russell Sage Foundation, 2001).

Wolff, Edward N., and Marcia Marley. "Long-Term Trends in U.S. Wealth Inequality: Methodological Issues and Results." In R. Lipsey and H. Tice, eds., *The Measurement of Saving, Investment, and Wealth, Studies of Income and Wealth,* vol. 52 (Chicago: University of Chicago Press, 1989): 765–839.

Index